WORKSHOP MODELS FOR FAMILY LIFE EDUCATION

AGING PARENTS: WHOSE RESPONSIBILITY?

Jane Goz Goodman

Family Service Association of America
44 East 23rd Street
New York, New York 10010

Library of Congress Cataloging in Publication Data

Goodman, Jane Goz.
    Aging parents.

    (Workshop models for family life education)
    Bibliography: p.
    1. Family life education--Handbooks, manuals, etc.
2. Aging--Handbooks, manuals, etc. 3. Parents--Hand-
books, manuals, etc. I. Title. II. Series.
HQ10.G65   306.8'7   80-14945
ISBN 0-87304-175-5

Printed in the U.S.A.

PREFACE

Workshop Models for Family Life Education is a series of manuals intended to promote the exploration of new alternatives and the utilization of new options in day-to-day living through programs in family life education.

Basically, family life education is a service of planned intervention that applies the dynamic process of group learning to improving the quality of individual and family living. The manuals are in workshop format and offer possible new approaches of service to families. They are meant to serve as a training mechanism and basic framework for group leaders involved in FLE workshops.

In 1974, the Family Service Association of America appointed a National Task Force on Family Life Education, Development, and Enrichment. One of the goals of the Task Force was to assess the importance and future direction of family life education services within family service agencies. One of the recommendations of their report was to "recognize family life education, development, and enrichment as one of the three major services of the family service agency: family counseling, family life education, and family advocacy."[1] This recommendation was adopted by the Board of Directors of FSAA and has become basic policy of the Association.

---

1. "Overview of Findings of the FSAA Task Force on Family Life Education, Development, and Enrichment" (New York: Family Service Association of America, May 1976), p. 21 (mimeographed).

iii

An interest in family life education is a natural development of FSAA's role in the strengthening of family life and complementary to the more traditional remedial functions of family agencies. FLE programs can add a new dimension to the services provided by family agencies. They can open an agency to the general population by providing programs which are appropriate for all families and individuals, not only for those at risk. They provide a new arena for service that deals with growth as well as dysfunction. They can encourage agencies to look beyond the therapeutic approach and to take on a new objective for the enrichment and strengthening of family life. For the participants, FLE programs can lead to increased understanding of normal stress, growth of esteem for one's self and others, development of communications skills, improved ability to cope with problem situations, development of problem-solving skills, and maximization of family and individual potential.

This series provides tangible evidence of FSAA's continuing interest in family life education and of a belief in its future importance for family services. FLE programs, coordinated within a total agency program and viewed as a vital and integral part of the agency, can become key factors in family service concern for growth and development within all families.

W. Keith Daugherty
General Director
Family Service Association
of America

TABLE OF CONTENTS

SESSION 3

SESSION 4

SESSION 5

FOREWORD

The Jewish Family and Children's Service (JFCS) of St. Louis,
Missouri, has had a long and active interest in prevention. Our
staff made educational groups available for members of the community
even prior to 1964, when the Family Service Association of America
and the Child Study Association of America co-sponsored a watershed
national project to train family caseworkers in the leadership of
parent education discussion groups.

The presence of a formal family life education program in a counseling
agency usually indicates that the agency's board of directors has gone
through a soul-searching process that has resulted in their commitment
to providing services not only for amelioration of manifest problems
in clients who seek out the agency, but also for the diminution of
disabling stress through helping people find better, more adaptive
ways to deal with life's inevitable changes. In essence, the board
has agreed that the agency's financial resources will be shared in
some proportion between prevention and treatment. Although the line
between the two is becoming more blurred for some of us as we strive
to master the skills each discipline requires, the bottom line still
remains: By investing in one you inevitably limit your ability to
provide maximum coverage for the other. Our agency, as many others
in the nation, has become convinced that a two-prong approach has
meaning and relevance for our mandate to provide services that will
enhance and strengthen family life.

Both sectarian and secular family agencies are very aware of how
vulnerable an institution the family has become and the great degree
of support from all quarters it requires in order to withstand the

fierce attacks that are being leveled against it. The philosophical underpinnings of family life education do not suggest that there is only one way to live, but indeed do affirm that the sustenance members provide each other is essential for the growing child's development and for adults faced with constantly changing mores and expectations. The material in this manual demonstrates that family life programming seeks to facilitate and promote the development of the individual's potential for satisfying and constructive living in terms of self-sufficiency and human relatedness. It allows for the exploration of new alternatives and for the utilization of a range of options in living. Sectarian agencies also believe that it is important to focus on how the issues at hand impinge on the family as a cohesive unit, and how it impacts on the family's commitment to religious and ethnic identity and continuity.

The humanness of the family life education approach and its commitment to the basic values of social work are not lost, but rather well-illustrated by this "how to do it" workshop model. Here an opportunity is afforded for adult children to discuss the nature of their unique relationships with their parents and to discover that, as they struggle with the universal difficulty inherent in "doing the right thing," they are not alone. There is an opportunity to sort out which behavior of their own helps things to go well and which actions seem to exacerbate the situation, how their spouses and other family members become a part of the problem or contribute to the solution. The leader's guided intervention (primarily along educational and clarifying lines) broadens their potential to see their relationships with their parents in less stereotyped ways. The leader "opens them up" to other possibilities. Other group members' problems and solutions illuminate their own concerns and encourage alternate ways of relating and helping.

All of us grow older and the older generation continues to grow in numbers--we are witnessing "the greying of America." Those families will be best served who are provided with perspectives that will help them appreciate and maximize the important roles their "senior family historians" can play and who can be clear-eyed about what aging vulnerable adults require, not only for physical health, but also in order to keep that rugged spark alive that helps us all maintain human connectedness and integrity.

Jane Goz Goodman, the author of this manual was one of the agency's early trainees in family life education. In March of 1977 she became Director of the Family Life Education program of Jewish Family and Children's Serivce. Later that year she participated and represented the agency at FSAA's first national symposium on Family Life Education Development and Enrichment in New Orleans. She has given dynamic leadership to the development of this program moving beyond the more typical focus on parent-child relationships to include various target populations among whom are the adult children and their aging parents she writes of here.

Jewish Family and Children's Service joins with the author in making this workshop model available with the hope that it will be of value to all who have undertaken the difficult but very gratifying task of aiding adult children and their parents to clear the way for mutual "caring and sharing"--those two human qualities that so frequently get lost in the everyday struggle to survive.

Harry Rubinstein
Executive Director
Jewish Family & Children's Service
St. Louis, Missouri

GENERAL INFORMATION
ABOUT THE WORKSHOP

It is suggested that you look over and familiarize yourself with the entire manual prior to beginning the workshop, paying particular attention to the general information about the workshop and the preparation sections that precede each session.

Before the start of each session, it is helpful to acquaint yourself thoroughly with the outline and material in that session and to prepare the handout and exercise material for the session. You may want to prepare notecards or flipcharts for the mini-lecture, and you may need to plan time to gather the suggested materials for each session.

Each of the sessions is planned as a continuation of the previous meeting and builds to and provides continuity for the session that follows. It is suggested that you follow the sessions as numbered, although you may wish to extend the more lengthy sessions to two sessions.

WHO COMES TO THESE WORKSHOPS? The people who come to our workshop are usually, but not always, middle-aged. In our workshop the members have always been female, which may be a confirmation of the hypothesis that caretakers of aging parents are traditionally female --daughter, daughter-in-law, granddaughter, niece, or aunt. The exclusively female attendance may also be related to the fact that the workshop was offered during the day. Other groups may find a balance of men and women in attendance.

Group members are usually struggling to maintain a balance between their own lives and the lives of their parents. They are in pain and are overwhelmed by feelings of guilt, anxiety, confusion, and anger. The material that is shared is emotionally laden, and the group quickly coalesces around the need to be understood and helped and the real wish to offer support and encouragement to each other.

Opening sessions in particular may be intense, tearful, and dramatic as members share their individual parental situations. The parents may be hospitalized and at the point of death; they may be at home but struggling with life-threatening illness and devastating pain; they may be in reasonably good health but becoming increasingly dependent emotionally. Or, some parents may be totally disoriented as the result of disease or neurological trauma.

PUBLICITY: This agency prepares a Family Life Education brochure twice a year, in fall and spring. The brochure includes a variety of offerings in addition to this workshop. A brief overview of each workshop is included in the brochure. The brochure is mailed to the active client list, the inactive client list of the past two years, all area doctors and lawyers, social workers in private practice, psychiatrists and psychoanalysts, clergy, community organizations such as community centers and counseling centers and family service agencies, all media sources (daily and neighborhood newspapers, television and radio stations), past workshop participants, all community persons who have expressed interest in our workshops, and schools (public and private).

In addition a memo is prepared for staff and accompanies the FLE brochure; it asks staff to go over their caseload to determine which,

6

if any, clients might benefit from the workshops offered. Staff are asked to talk to such clients and make referrals to the groups as appropriate.

Agency staff appear on television talk shows and radio stations. Brochures are placed in supermarkets, churches, synagogues, and court-houses. Synagogues and churches are requested to print information about the workshops in their weekly bulletins.

In addition to the FLE brochure, individual flyers or press releases should be prepared for each workshop for the community news sections of each newspaper and for public service announcements on television and radio.

About two weeks prior to the start of each workshop, the leader should send a letter to or telephone each registrant, saying that you are looking forward to her participation in the group, giving directions to the agency, parking information, and restating the dates and times of the workshop.

SIZE OF THE GROUPS: We have found that the best-sized group is one of between eight and twelve people. You may have a very good group of somewhat less than eight, but if you have a group larger than twelve persons, you will have to eliminate many of the go-rounds and shorten the discussion periods.

NUMBER OF SESSIONS: Our workshops consist of six sessions, although you can extend the material to eight or even ten sessions, particularly if you have a large group.

LENGTH OF SESSIONS: Although each of the sessions is planned for one-and-one-half hours, you may find that you need two hours to complete the material. The time allotment for each session is to be used as a guide and is based upon a 90-minute session. Again, mold the manual to your own requirements and style and plan time accordingly. Sessions lasting longer than two hours should be avoided.

TECHNIQUES: The workshop utilizes: mini-lectures, discussion, role plays, values clarification exercises, and handout materials.

OUTLINE AND OBJECTIVE: There is a detailed outline for each session, with an objective listed for the leader's use in guiding and focusing the session.

PREPARATION NOTES: The preparation notes for each session are divided into three parts: setting the stage, materials needed, and time allotment.

Read through the preparation section for each session prior to the beginning of the workshop. Session 5 requires that you secure a packet of pamphlets of community resources well in advance (see page 125). The materials required for any session are easily obtained and relatively inexpensive.

WELCOME AND UPDATE: You will note that we include a Welcome and Update at the beginning of each session. This is an important part of the session because it allows each member to provide an update on the parental situation and to note any changes. Because this kind of group becomes cohesive and supportive in the first session, the members are interested in exchanging information about how parents

are faring and how the adult children are coping. Always allow suf-
ficient time for each member to update each week.

MINI-LECTURES: The mini-lectures can be presented informally and in
your own words. You may want to jot a few key words on notecards as
a guide, or you may want to make an outline of your mini-lecture on
the blackboard or flipchart so that the group can follow along as you
speak. You may choose to have some discussion during the mini-
lecture, or you may opt to hold discussion until you are finished.

HANDOUTS: These are listed in the Outline for each session and again
in the preparation notes for each session.

CLOSURE: It is important to bring the group to closure at each
session. You may find that one or two members need to talk to you
for a few minutes after each session and, if possible, do not schedule
anything immediately following the session so that you can be
available.

SESSION 1

SESSION 1

BRIEF OUTLINE

OBJECTIVE: To introduce each member to the group.
To help each member articulate where she or he is in the parental relationship.

PREPARATION

A. Setting the Stage
B. Materials Needed
C. Time Allotment

I. INTRODUCTION--GETTING ACQUAINTED

A. Leader and Member Go-round
B. Statement and Purpose of the Workshop
C. Overview and Ground Rules
D. Brief Statement of the Policy and Services of the Sponsoring Agency

II. GOAL SETTING

Extended Name Cards

III. VALUES CLARIFICATION EXERCISES

IV. DETERMINING THE EXTENT OF YOUR RESPONSIBILITY TO
     YOUR PARENT

     A. Mini-lecture
     B. Discussion

V. HANDOUTS

SESSION 1

PREPARATION

A. Setting the Stage

1. Providing a comfortable room with good lighting, adequate
ventilation, temperature control, and chairs arranged around a
table creates an atmosphere conducive to discussion and learning.
It is preferable to meet in the same room for each of the sessions. Providing coffee is an ice-breaker and an identifiable
amenity.

Members may arrive ten to fifteen minutes before the session
begins. Use this time to welcome each person informally.

Some members may be first-timers, some may be current or past
clients of the agency, some may be former workshop members, or
some may be known to you through the community. At this first
session using name tags can be helpful. Once the group is
assembled and seated, you may find that noting on paper the names
and seating arrangement, perhaps with a descriptive word or two
about each member will help you to remember each one's name.
Because group members tend to sit in the same seats throughout
the workshop, this noting of names and seats can provide a simple
mnemonic device for you.

If you charge a fee and have not collected all of the fees in
advance, you may complete fee collection before the start of the
session.

2. Prepare the handouts

B. Materials Needed for Session 1

1. Name tags and felt tip markers
2. 8" x 5" index cards
3. Paper and pencils
4. Flipchart or blackboard
5. Agency brochures (if you plan to discuss the sponsoring agency)
6. A clock or watch so that you can begin and end on time

C. Time Allotment for Session 1

This is a rough estimate of how the time may be spent. You may find that you follow the suggested times, or you may find yourself spending twice as much time on the goal setting section, much less on the discussion period. Again, this time allotment is meant to be used only as a guide. The sessions are one and one-half hours in length; the suggested material for each session can usually be covered in this time.

I.	Introduction	20 minutes
II.	Goal Setting	20 minutes
III.	Values Clarification Exercises	10 minutes
IV.	Mini-lecture	15 minutes
	Discussion	20 minutes
V.	Handout and Closure	5 minutes
		90 minutes

SESSION 1

I. INTRODUCTION--GETTING ACQUAINTED

A. Leader and Member Go-round

1. Leader introduces self

By introducing yourself first you set the stage and make it easier for the members to talk about themselves. After welcoming the group, identify yourself briefly on two levels--professionally, and as an adult child who has coped with various problems related to parental relationships. Members want to know your credentials and potential for understanding their problems before revealing themselves in the group.

2. Introduction of members

After you introduce yourself, ask the member on your left to continue by giving his or her name and telling something about him or herself and the parental situation. Acknowledge the member's introduction by nodding, saying "okay," or "thank you," and in a clockwise rotation ask the next participant to continue.

This introductory go-round can be an intense, emotionally laden, and tear-producing experience as group members share their current life situations with sick or dying parents, or healthy but demanding parents. Members may be feeling overwhelmed with feelings of guilt, anger, fear, and confusion. At the conclusion of this go-round you may notice that:

(a) The group has begun to develop a sense of cohesiveness based on the shared material.

(b) The members are beginning the unburdening process by articulating and acknowledging the problem.

(c) The members quickly become vocal participants during the go-round, even shy members gain confidence by hearing the sound of their own voices.

(d) The members begin to acknowledge a feeling of support from the group as well as a genuine concern for the others in the group. There is almost always some brief supportive group interchange as the members are introducing themselves.

(e) Without exception, there is a shared feeling of relief best expressed as, "I didn't know anyone else was going through this!"

B. Statement and Purpose of Workshop
Acknowledge the feelings expressed.

"The purpose of this workshop is to learn new ways of coping with and understanding our relationship to our parents. Because we have a unique and long history as children to our parents, we will examine the nature of that special and sometimes painful relationship in determining the extent and quality of our responsibility to our parents.

"We will refer to the special relationship of children to parents as filial maturity, a concept which we will explore and define throughout this workshop."

C. Overview and Ground Rules

"Our workshop is not intended to provide therapy. The
emphasis will be on learning new coping skills and understanding normative behavior and normative life crises; one
of which is being faced with responsibility for our parents
and trying to determine the extent and quality of that
responsibility. We will be talking about where we are in
the parental relationship, how we got there, and how we
can make it better. We will discuss the importance of
meeting our own needs and the concept of filial maturity.
We will talk about what our parents can expect from us, and
what we can reasonably expect from our parents. We will
look at the physical and emotional aspects of the aging
process and explore the local community resources that are
available for planning support systems for our parents.
Throughout we'll be talking about feelings such as anger,
guilt, and fear.

"To make certain that each group member has an opportunity
to have their questions answered, and to learn individual
needs, I will be asking for your input today in what I call
goals collection. These goals will be combined on a flipchart which I will prepare for the next session. We will go
over this chart in the second session, and again in the last
session so that we can determine how successfully your goals
have been met. This is an open group, and you are encouraged
to participate fully with your comments and questions.

"In this workshop we will utilize: discussions, mini-
lectures, values clarification exercises, handouts, flipcharts

and role plays.

"Our ground rules usually include the following:
1. "Members are expected to attend all six sessions. If you cannot attend, please let me know as much in advance as possible.
2. "Material shared by group members is confidential.
3. "For those members who miss a session, I will provide a 'catch-up' session about 15 minutes prior to the following session. This session will be by appointment.
4. "Any changes in scheduling because of holidays, or conflict with major community functions can be negotiated by the group.
5. "If new members want to join the group by the second session, but no later than that, the group will make the decision about taking them in.
6. "The issue of smoking will be decided by the group." If the group decides on a non-smoking rule, allow time for smokebreaks.

D. Brief Statement of the Policy and Services of the Sponsoring Agency
This can be done by distributing agency brochures, and briefly mentioning the agency's major service programs. This is an invaluable public relations statement for the agency and members are generally curious about the agency's programs and often unaware of the many services available.

II. GOAL SETTING

A. Extended Name Cards

1. Distribute the 8" x 5" index cards and pencils or pens. Explain that you will be collecting the completed cards to use in preparing several flip charts for use in the workshop. As you give directions for the card, you may either prepare yours and hold it up as a guide, or prepare a sample on the blackboard or flipchart:

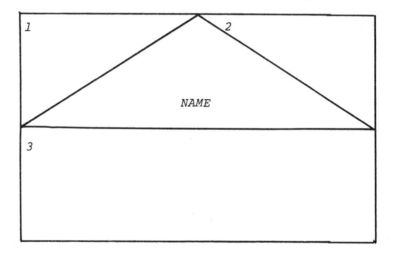

2. "Draw lines on your cards similar to the ones on the sample. Write your name in the triangle and number the sections of the card as indicated."
3. "In section 1 list in several brief phrases what you can reasonably expect of your parents."
4. "In section 2 list in several brief phrases what your parents can reasonably expect from you."
5. "In section 3 list what you want to achieve from this workshop experience; what your goals and needs are."

6. "On the back of the card list your wishes and fantasies." This has been found to be facilitating inasmuch as it provides an acknowledged fantasy alternative to an often grim reality. It does not obliterate the reality in any way but seems rather, to make the reality more tolerable and acceptable.

7. Ask members to leave the extended name cards with you at the close of the session to help you compile the list of goals for the next session. Also, explain that you will attempt to incorporate these goals and needs into the future sessions.

III. VALUES CLARIFICATION EXERCISES

At this point in the session, it is usually a good idea to introduce a couple of exercises which quickly focus on how the members feel about aging. One exercise, "Being Old Means . . ." will do that, and it is used in the first session as a way of assessing where the group is. The second exercise, using the hand normally not used for writing, gives a quick and dramatic awareness of one of the myriad problems which creates frustration for the aging.

A. Exercise One--Being Old Means . . .
   You may do this in several ways, as a verbal go-round, as a written exercise, or you may write the responses on a blackboard or flipchart. Doing a verbal go-round seems to get the most accurate-feeling responses. Usual responses include:
   1. "Being old means . . ."
      Sick
      Unattractive
      Helpless
      Poor
      Senile
      Out of control
      Loneliness
      Deterioration
      Impending death
      Dependency
   2. Discussion
      Spend a few minutes discussing the group members'

responses and note, if the group's responses are
similar to those above, that there may be no positives
in the list. Solicit the group's reactions to this.

B. Exercise Two--Alternate Hand
    1. Distribute paper and pencils.
    2. Ask the group to write the following with the hand they
        do not normally use:
        a. Their name
        b. Today's date
        c. Their address
        This is sufficient to have each member sense the
        frustration of attempting a skill once mastered, but
        now unmanageable.
    3. Discussion
        You may want to spend a few minutes discussing their
        reactions and feelings before moving to the mini-
        lecture. Some typical responses when asked how it
        feels to attempt this exercise are:
        a. Shaky
        b. Inadequate
        c. Nervous
        d. Tense
        e. Angry
        f. Impatient
        g. "My body was betraying me"
        h. Embarrassed

IV. DETERMINING THE EXTENT OF YOUR RESPONSIBILITY

A. Mini-lecture

"When we think about our parents and try to determine the
extent of our responsibility for them, we are often con-
flicted because of our struggle to meet our own needs, our
immediate family's needs, and the needs of our parents.
This dilemma is sometimes handled by doing too little, which
results in guilt feelings; or by doing too much (at the
expense of your own and immediate family's needs), which
results in expressed or unexpressed anger and resentment;
or, the conflict may be so powerful that it immobilizes
and obviates any action. In each of these three possible
ways to handle parents' needs, ultimately no one's needs are
really met; there is pain, confusion, anger, guilt, and
resentment.

"Before we can determine the extent of our responsibility
toward our parents, several things need to be worked
through. First, we need to feel that we are okay and that
it is all right to meet our own needs. We need to have a
relationship with our parents that permits us to relate to
them out of love and care as an adult child to parent, not
out of anger or fear.

"As I listen to you today talking about your life situations with your parents, I hear that you are concerned,
that you do care about your parents, but that you are also
frightened by the changes which you see taking place in
parents who, for most of your life, were strong and powerful

25

and in a more independent, authoritarian position in relationship to you. There is, of course, something frightening
about the changes you have been describing. Some of your
parents are experiencing the beginning of the aging process
with minimal change in function; others are watching
parents struggle with devastating, and perhaps life-
threatening, illness and pain; and several have parents
who are experiencing loss of memory, disordered thinking,
and faulty reasoning, all of which are particularly painful
to observe.

"As young children who have parents and grandparents, aunts
and uncles, we have a sense, almost, of immortality, sur-
rounded by so many strong caring adults. It seems as though
most children share a common fantasy that they will never
die, that perhaps 'others' may die, but not they. Many of
you may have experienced a similar childhood feeling.

"As we grow up and begin to experience losses, we are
sobered by the reality that loved ones do die and that perhaps we too will someday die. This is a process which most
of us go through. In a way, as long as one's parents or
grandparents are alive, we are not on the 'front line' of
mortality, but are behind the lines, protected and less
vulnerable to death. As parents age, become ill, perhaps
die, our vulnerability is exposed, we are pushed closer
to the 'front line' and we experience uneasy feelings
about our own mortality.

"Seeing our parents age, become ill, lose sensory faculties, and become unable to care for themselves is frightening to us. We are unprepared for coping with our own painful feelings of impending loss and being pushed to that 'front line'. These uneasy feelings, together with the changes our parents may be experiencing often make the adult-child/parent relationship painful and nonproductive.

"What we want to do during this workshop is to try to understand the dynamics of this relationship and begin to work toward feeling better about ourselves, to become more understanding of our parents' struggles and problems, and to make some concrete decisions about how we can improve that relationship, be helpful to our parents, and, in the process, teach this to our own children.

"Every advanced religious and ethical concept demands that we honor the aged. We do indeed have a responsibility toward our parents, but that the extent of that responsibility is determined by you, your family, and your parents. Before you can work out your own 'formula' for this you must become aware of and recognize your own needs; come to terms with those needs; and meet those needs as far as possible.

"It is moral, ethical, legal and all right to meet your own needs, and it is essential to your fulfillment as a human being to do so. If you give up meeting your own needs consistently you will feel angry, guilty, helpless, or sick.

"In determining the extent of your responsibility you must
first determine with your parents (assuming this is possible) what needs to be done and what their preferences
are. Then, meet with all of the members in your family to
plan for and to share the responsibility. If you are an
only child or an only child in the area your parents live
in you'll need to involve surrogate family. Surrogates
can be neighbors, friends, volunteers, professionals, or
paid helpers. Again, it is very important to remember
that parents' needs, as they see them, are taken into
account in planning. Very often, in families with seven
or eight adult children, the responsibility for caring for
the parents falls on one adult child. In almost all cases,
the 'caretaker' child is female. Traditionally, we all
think in terms of females in caring roles, whether it's
daughter, sister, niece, or daughter-in-law. Broaden your
vision and begin to think in terms of including all family
members (or surrogates) in sharing the responsibility for
parents' care. In situations in which parents could live
in their own homes with the aid of a family or surrogate
support system, make a list of exactly what will be required
and then have a family meeting to work out the details.

"For example, an only child, who lived forty-five minutes
from her parents, worked out a plan with a neighbor, a
cousin, and a paid high school student to provide additional
support so that she would not have to make daily trips to
her parents' home. In another situation, a parent living
with an adult child with six siblings in the same city,
worked out an arrangement for the siblings to care for the

mother on an alternating schedule while the group member had a 'day out' each week. This extended family support system allowed this woman the first vacation she and her husband had taken in ten years.

"On another level, some of you have described problems with physically and intellectually intact parents, who live in their own homes, but who have over the years developed a stronger and more intense pattern of emotional dependence on you which is becoming overwhelming. For instance, the first telephone call of the day from mother is early morning, followed by three or four additional calls throughout the day. You may feel guilty if your parents maintain keys to your home and they use the keys inappropriately. Your parents may interfere with grandchildren.

"In any event, as we consider the variety of situations with your parents which brought you here today, whether your parents are aging noticeably with physical and sensory problems, whether they are physically well, but emotionally more dependent on you, whatever the particulars may be in any situation, you are here today because your relationship and responsibility to your aging parents is changing and causing pain to you and to your parents. How you determine the extent of your responsibility, or to put it another way, how you resolve the total relationship to your parents is our task in this workshop. We will not provide a magical formula for each of you, but we will attempt to consider the dynamics of the adult child-parent relationship and offer some suggestions for options, choices, better

understanding, and alternate coping solutions. Many of
the coping solutions and insights into understanding will
come from the group as we work together."

B. Discussion

Following the mini-lecture briefly discuss the material
covered. Continue the discussion until about five minutes
before the close of the session.

V. HANDOUTS

Distribute copies of the handout for Session 1 (see page 35) and copies of the bibliography on aging (see pages 165-68).

HANDOUT

FOR

SESSION 1

KEY POINTS OF THE MINI-LECTURE

DETERMINING THE EXTENT OF YOUR RESPONSIBILITY TO YOUR PARENTS

1. We do indeed have a responsibility toward our parents, but a responsibility that is evolved and redefined by working through the old relationship which may have been painful and nonproductive, and arriving at a new relationship based on love, understanding, and self-acceptance.

2. Responsibility for parents is best met as a shared responsibility, either with other family members or with surrogate family: paid helpers, volunteers, neighbors, professionals, and community resources.

3. Parents' wishes and needs must be considered and be part of any planning on their behalf.

4. We need to be cognizant of our own needs and learn not to feel guilty when we take care of ourselves.

5. It is moral, ethical, and legal to meet your own needs.

6. If you give up meeting your needs <u>consistently</u> you will feel angry, guilty, helpless, or sick.

SESSION 2

SESSION 2

BRIEF OUTLINE

OBJECTIVE: To help the group understand the dynamics of the parent-child relationship and to evaluate the potential for change.

PREPARATION

    A. Setting the Stage
    B. Materials Needed
    C. Time Allotment

I. WELCOME AND UPDATE

II. GOALS FLIPCHART

    A. Sample Chart
    B. Role Play

III. WHAT CAN I REASONABLY EXPECT OF MY PARENTS?

    A. Sample Chart
    B. Role Play

IV. FILIAL MATURITY

    A. Mini-lecture
    B. Discussion

V. HANDOUTS

SESSION 2

PREPARATION

A. <u>Setting the Stage</u>
   1. Prepare a goals flipchart from the first session's extended name cards. Many of the responses on the cards will be similar; combine those but also include the extraneous goals so that members feel that what they want is important and is not overlooked.
   2. Prepare a flipchart on "What can I reasonably expect of my Parents," from the material in the extended name cards.
   3. Prepare the handouts which you want to distribute. You might choose the goals flipchart and the key points of the mini-lecture.

B. <u>Materials Needed</u>
   Paper and pencils

C. <u>Time Allotment</u>

I.	Welcome and Update	10 minutes
II.	Goals Flipchart (discussion and role play)	30 minutes
III.	"What Can I Reasonably Expect of My Parents?" (discussion and role play)	30 minutes
IV.	Mini-lecture--Filial Maturity	15 minutes
V.	Handouts	5 minutes
		90 minutes

SESSION 2

I. WELCOME AND UPDATE

A very brief social exchange may be helpful in establishing
relationships with members who are shy or extremely anxious.

Ask if there are any comments or reactions to last week's session. Ask members to provide an "update" on their parental
situation, usually they will indicate a positive change or
move, but they may indicate an exacerbation of the situation.
It is important to provide time at the beginning of each session
for this "update." Occasionally, a member's parent will die
during the course of a workshop, and frequently a parent will be
hospitalized. The group provides a great deal of strength and
support in those situations, and becomes in many ways a surrogate
family to the member.

The mini-lecture for this session covers the basic themes and
issues which are dealt with in the discussion and role plays
on the "goals" flipchart, and the "What Can I Reasonably Expect
of My Parents?" flipchart. You may choose to go ahead with a
focused and germane discussion and not use the mini-lecture.
Or, you may prefer to utilize the structured mini-lecture and
limit discussion accordingly. In either mode, the same ground
may be quite adequately covered.

II. GOALS FLIPCHART

Go over each item on the flipchart with the group. Note that most of the group had similar concerns and issues relating to: feelings, the reality issues of aging, and a need to acquire specific and concrete information. There will be some discussion as you go over the list.

A. Sample Goals Chart

To learn how to cope with the guilt.

To overcome the anger associated with the responsibility toward my parents.

To learn how to communicate, how to talk to my parents, say what I'm feeling without crying, screaming, or getting angry.

To get help in learning to resolve conflicts, to forgive each other and not harbor deep intense resentment.

To learn if my parents love me and approve of me.

To learn how to cope with my own needs and my parents' needs and be fair in prioritizing.

To learn how to help my parents be as independent as possible.

To be more patient and less short-tempered with my parents.

To clarify the whole issue of responsibility--whose is it?

To learn more about the process of aging.

What are the community resources, particularly nursing homes, and how do I choose a good one?

How can I have privacy when my parent lives with me?

B. Role Plays

This is an appropriate time to do some role playing based
on input from members. You may choose not to utilize role
plays at this time, or to use them briefly, or to spend
some time giving the group an opportunity to work on
individual problems. Be sensitive to the discussion and
be able to say, "I wonder if it would help to role play what
you're sharing?" Your group may accept this as a mode of
problem solving and offer vignettes for the group to role
play. The efficacy of such role play is that the member who
suggests the vignette gets actual practice in changing her
or his behavior and the others have an opportunity to hear
and learn from it.

1. A woman is feeling overwhelmed, angry, and guilty because her parents always arrange their doctor's appointments at a time that is inconvenient for the daughter
who takes them to these appointments.

Ask for volunteers to play mother and daughter. If the
group is reluctant to try this, you may offer to play
the daughter and select a member who may have a similar
problem to play the mother. Solutions are usually
forthcoming which include a recognition of the parents'
feelings and needs as well as the adult child's needs
and rights. The adult child may say that she is not
free on Tuesdays and Thursdays but it's fine to make
appointments on Mondays and Wednesdays and Friday would
be all right in a pinch.

The concept of limit setting is introduced. Many group members may be surprised by this role play and feel encouraged to consider new ways of solving problems. The daughter might also offer to take her parents to lunch prior to the doctor's appointment. This reflects the adult child's limit setting on days and on the adult child's recognition of her own rights.

2. An eighty-year-old woman who lives with her daughter: the daughter's life had begun to revolve around physical care for her mother, including preparing meals, cutting food and providing a warm beverage at lunchtime. This routine prevented the adult child from leaving her home for a luncheon date or for other activities. The role play provided a solution: preparing a warm beverage and placing it in a thermos and preparing food that required no cutting, or was pre-cut. The daughter was supported in her need to care for her mother, but was encouraged to meet her own needs as well.

3. An active and busy adult child who enjoyed many activities, such as tennis, golf, organizational work, and meeting with friends felt guilty. Her parents lived in their own home, were reasonably well physically, and had no financial problems. The adult child was feeling guilty and angry, however, because her mother called her early each morning to ask what she was doing that day, and then her mother would say that she was lonely and miserable and had no friends. The mother did not ask the daughter to do anything concrete,

but the adult child felt guilty, miserable, and angry.
In the role play the adult child responded to mother by
saying:

"I'm really looking forward to my game of tennis
today. The exercise is good for me and it's fun to
be with my foursome."

"I'm really feeling good about being able to do this
since the kids are on their own at last, and I can
enjoy doing what I like. I've earned the right to
my freedom."

"You sound lonely Mom, would you like to have lunch
and shop on Thursday?"

"I wonder if you'd like to visit the community
center (or similar group) and see what's available
for you? I'd really like to know that you were
spending some of your time with your own friends and
doing things you like, but I really like to spend
time with you myself."

4. The adult child's overconcern when she visited her
   parents' home and found that their refrigerator was not
   as full as she thought it should be. This role play
   pointed up that the adult child was **overreacting not**
   to the reality, but to her own feelings of guilt about
   not doing enough.

III. WHAT CAN I REASONABLY EXPECT OF MY PARENTS?

Discuss the items on the flipchart which you have prepared from your group's extended name cards. Or, provide copies of the flipchart material for each member. Using the material on a flipchart stimulates spirited discussion which might take the place of the mini-lecture.

A. <u>Sample Chart</u>
   Understanding of my needs and responsibilities
   Help with the housework within her ability (for parent living with adult child)
   To be as independent as possible for as long as possible
   To love me and not be critical or disapproving of me and my family's lifestyle
   To not make me feel guilty when I must say "no"
   Financial support if I need it and they can give it
   To hear my problems and give me advice
   That they will let me know when they really need me in emergencies and not keep "secrets" from me regarding health problems or major concern while occasionally telling these "secrets" to others
   That they will at times be sick, that they will age and experience sensory loss
   Love and friendship
   They will make demands on me
   Not to manipulate me and my family
   To be a positive part of my family and our life
   Consideration, respect, and acceptance
   To be courteous

That they will be well-groomed and make a nice appearance
That they will maintain a social life as much as possible
and not depend on me to fulfill all of their social needs
That they respect my privacy
That they occasionally use the bus with their friends
That they love me as much as my siblings and not show
favoritism, or play us against each other

B. Role Plays

 1. The adult child and her widowed father who lived alone
    but maintained a key to his adult child's home: The
    father was using his key inappropriately, for instance,
    by coming in when no one was at home and opening the
    mail. This created much ill will, which the daughter
    could not articulate to her father. In the role play
    the adult child asked her father to come over to have
    coffee and talk about something that was bothering her.
    She said that she wanted her father to have a key to
    her home, but she was feeling edgy because her father
    never called before coming over and came at all hours
    without letting her know. She also said that she did
    not want him to open her family's mail because this
    took away their privacy. The daughter wanted her
    father to call her before coming over, but asked how
    he would feel about this. The father in the role play
    got angry and said that he didn't need to call before
    visiting his child's home. The daughter said that
    she understood how he was feeling but that she was not
    just his "child," but a grown woman, wife, and mother,
    who had feelings and rights of her own. She said that

she loved her father but wanted them to be honest with
each other and have a good relationship based on
understanding and respect.

The group members may respond strongly to this role
play by saying that they often want to tell their
parents how they feel, but that they could not for
fear of their parents' wrath. The role play may bring
out many issues for examination and clarification.
One basic theme in these role play experiences is the
fundamental that, if the adult child is feeling
reasonably good about herself, or okay, there is less
defensiveness and anger in her responses to her
parents.

Another point to emphasize is that alternate solutions
and new coping skills can be found if one begins to
think in such terms. You can also place emphasis on
looking for the reasons that seemingly thoughtless
or selfish requests and demands, and with that understanding to react to the parent more lovingly and
kindly.

The discussions on the role play are significant,
insightful, and educational. Members will refer back
to role play situations and talk about the positive
and good changes they have felt strong enough to make
as a result of being able to act out the problem
situation. The solutions offered by the group in this
last role play situation included an acceptance of the

father's needs, his loneliness, concerns about losing power and control over his adult child, and some fears of his own death. These were balanced against the adult child's needs to assert herself as a loving daughter, but also as an adult who had boundaries and rights and could set limits.

2. Parents are angry because the adult child did not invite a certain distant relative to a family gathering. This role play points up control issues, and some limit setting. Played out with love and respect for the parents, it emphasizes the adult child's rights to plan her own guest list even though it might not meet her parents' approval. Many unresolved issues between the parent and adult child relate to the issues of approval, acceptance, and validation. Many group members may never quite feel that they have measured up to their parents' expectations.

3. Another type of role play can involve the parent who has thought disorder or memory loss. This is particularly painful and the role play provides group members with an opportunity to express their pain and fear that the once-strong independent parent is failing.

It may also point up some concrete ways of responding. For instance, the parent who no longer recognizes the adult child by name and refers to her by his dead wife's name may stir up very painful feelings

in the adult child.   In the role play the adult child
is encouraged to respond lovingly without insisting on
establishing her own identity.   This role play
relieves the adult child of some pain and anxiety and
offers a simple but concrete suggestion for relating.

IV. FILIAL MATURITY

A. <u>Mini-lecture</u>

"The term "filial" denotes the relationship of a child to
its parent. The term <u>filial maturity</u> implies that as in
other life tasks which we must master, we come finally to
a relationship with our parents in which we relate not as
dependent child to parent, nor as parent to our parents,
but as adult children to our parents. Some of our life
tasks are learning to walk, talk, master certain learning
skills, achieving independence, achieving self-identity,
sexual maturity and responsibility, marrying, bearing
children, pursuing careers, experiencing being part of a
family and a friendship, mastering losses, and finally
being able to face our own death.

"Very little is offered in the literature to tell us about
achieving and mastering the life task of filial maturity.
We read and hear that what occurs as adult children are
faced with caring for their aging parents is a <u>role
reversal</u> in which the adult children become parents to
their parents. This is an untenable position. Because
of the dynamics of the child-parent relationship, reversing
roles and assuming the parenting of your parents may be
fraught with difficulties and temptations to 'get back' at
or retaliate against 'helpless' parents for what is re-
called and perceived as poor, deficient, and perhaps cruel
parenting.

"All children feel frustrated occasionally as parents exert control over their lives, their destiny, and their wishes. Most adults can recall instances in their early lives in which their parents forbade them to attend the college of their choice, favored another sibling over them, did not approve of or validate them as worthwhile, refused to have them date or marry whom they wished, forced them into careers not of their choice, refused financial or emotional help when it was requested, perhaps deserted or abused them, divorced, did not express interest in their lives, and, in general, were restrictive or manipulative. The most painful memory seems to be that the parent failed to give the adult child a sense of worth, self-esteem, and self-confidence. Clearly, there are notable and frequent exceptions to these negative memories. Sometimes, however, these early experiences may have been buried for years but create present unexplained anger or resentment. The temptation as an adult child may be to vent such angry or resentful feelings on a parent who is aging and deteriorating.

"As our parents age, decline, lose power and control, we may have many conflicting feelings about what is happening. We may be fully aware of these conflicting feelings, or, we may be aware of only some and the others remain as unconscious feelings. As young children, we look to our parents as authority figures who are powerful, controlling, capable, strong, independent, caretaking, capable of giving or withholding love and esteem, and, in general, who are our loving protectors and guardians. As we achieve

adulthood this relationship and our perception of our
parents' power gradually changes. As our parents age
and approach the end of their lives, we may become
frightened and upset at the impending loss of our once
protective and loving and powerful parents, as well as
being pushed to take a look at our own mortality.

"In addition, we grow up and assume certain responsibilities not only for ourselves but for our own families;
our husbands, children and perhaps grandchildren. Most of
you are in the 'middle-age crunch'--you are still bearing
responsibility not only for your own children, but you
are being faced also with increasing responsibility for
your parents. Today's children often attend school for
more years than their parents and are still financially
and emotionally dependent on them, sometime through their
twenties. The lifestyle of today sets us up to be sand-
wiched or 'crunched' between two sets of responsibilities.

"Now we come to the adult child to parent relationship
filial maturity; a life task in which adults learn to
relate to their parents not as children, or as parents to
their parents, but as adult children to their parents.
Persons who have achieved filial maturity can hold their
own, meet their own needs, set proper limits, and give
real help to their parents without feeling overwhelmed or
overpowered. At the same time, persons who have achieved
filial maturity can finally forgive their parents, recognize their parents' needs, and accept their parents as
adult human beings. As in the mastery of other life tasks,

the achievement of filial maturity requires effort, understanding, patience, trial and error, self-acceptance, and
self-evaluation."

B. Discussion

Discussion in any group is always unique, but will probably
cover the same issues and move toward the development of
similar major themes. The quality of the discussion
depends on the past experiences of the group, how they
feel about sharing those experiences, and how effectively
they can be encouraged to participate. Discussion following this mini-lecture is spirited, lively, and replete
with shared reminiscences and recall relating to the filial
relationship.

V. HANDOUTS

Distribute copies of:

A. Goals Flipchart, page 43
B. Flipchart on "What Can I Reasonably Expect of My Parents,"
    page 47
C. Key Points on the Mini-lecture on Filial Maturity, page 59

HANDOUT

FOR

SESSION 2

FILIAL MATURITY

Filial maturity is a life task in which the adult child learns to relate to the parent not as a child to parent, nor as a parent to parent, but as an adult child to parent.

A person who has achieved this stage can hold her own, meet her own needs, set proper limits and give real help to her parents without feeling overwhelmed or overpowered.

At the same time, a person who has achieved filial maturity can finally forgive her parents, recognize the needs of her parents and accept her parents as adult human beings.

As in the mastery of other life tasks, the achievement of life tasks, the achievement of filial maturity requires effort, understanding, patience, trial and error, self-acceptance, and self-evaluation.

SESSION 3

SESSION 3

BRIEF OUTLINE

OBJECTIVE: To emphasize the importance of self-acceptance and the legitimacy of needs.

PREPARATION

    A. Setting the Stage
    B. Materials Needed
    C. Time Allotment

I. WELCOME AND UPDATE

II. WHAT MY PARENTS CAN REASONABLY EXPECT FROM ME

    A. Sample Flipchart
    B. Discussion and Role Play Suggestions

III. VALUES CLARIFICATION EXERCISES

    A. Reality Time Pie
    B. Fantasy Time Pie
    C. Life Line
    D. Basic Needs

IV. HOW TO BE A HAPPY AND SUCCESSFUL ADULT CHILD TO YOUR PARENT

   A. Mini-lecture
   B. Discussion

V. HOME ASSIGNMENT

   HANDOUTS

SESSION 3

PREPARATION

A. <u>Setting the Stage</u>
1. Prepare a flipchart from the material on the extended name cards, "What Can My Parents Reasonably Expect of Me?"
2. Prepare copies of handouts.
3. Select the values clarification exercises you wish to use from those suggested.

B. <u>Materials Needed</u>
1. Paper and pencils
2. 5" x 8" cards

C. <u>Time Allotment</u>

I.	Welcome and Update	10 minutes
II.	"What My Parents Can Reasonably Expect From Me (flipchart, presentation, discussion, and role play)	20 minutes
III.	Values Clarification Exercises	30 minutes
IV.	Mini-lecture	25 minutes
V.	Home Assignment	<u>5 minutes</u>
		90 minutes

SESSION 3

I. WELCOME AND UPDATE

Welcome members and ask how things are going in their lives.
Members will be eager to share changes. Time needs to be
allotted to this part of the session. Here are some typical
responses given at this point in the workshop:

"I'm not as anxious and guilt-ridden when I visit my
parents, . . . if their refrigerator isn't as full as I
think it should be I don't get into an argument over
it, . . . I'm relaxing more and feeling better about
myself."

"Since we began this group we received validation that
gave us the courage to make changes and do things in a
positive way."

"I have learned to stop infantilizing my parents and have
begun to see them as human beings."

"When my mother (who is senile) keeps asking about dead
relatives I no longer tell her they're dead and get angry
and provoked that she can't remember that, . . . instead
I'm able to say that they're fine and busy. This makes
her happy and I sure feel better."

"I've stopped encouraging my mother to get me to spend my
days off with her. I found out that she's pretty busy with
her own work and life, and I was feeling guilty that I
didn't spend all of my free time with her. I found out
that I don't have to do this, and now we both enjoy the
time we do decide to spend together."

"I found out that I have rights! I am beginning to recognize my needs <u>without</u> moving into a self-centered selfish position and without ignoring my parents' needs."

II. WHAT CAN MY PARENTS REASONABLY EXPECT FROM ME?

Put up the flipchart which you have prepared from the group's extended name cards. Explain to the group that you prepared the chart from their comments, and read through the entire list and discuss, or read the chart point-by-point and discuss each point individually.

A. Sample Flipchart

Love and understanding

Physical comforts and care

Consideration

Respect

Cooperation

Help with their problems

My time (within appropriate limits)

As much financial help as I can give if necessary

That they will be included as part of our family

Taking them to appointments, marketing, shopping

To come to my home on a regular basis, and take part
in family celebrations and holidays

That I will be responsive to their emergencies

That I will help them do the things they can no longer do
for themselves

To have fun with them, to listen and to see that they
remain as independent as possible

That I will attempt to balance my lifestyle and my time so
that I meet my needs and when I am with my parents I will
not feel resentful, angry, and sullen

That I will express my appreciation to them when they are
helpful
To be sensitive to their cues about how much help to offer
and when
To encourage my parents to communicate with me and not hold
back out of a fear of intruding upon my life
As much care and love as I want from my children

B. Discussion and Role Play

Discussion will be centered on the push-pull of the parental
relationship. Members relate to the old feelings about
parents that continually interfere with the current relationships.

1. Role Play

Ask group members for suggestions for role playing. Use
the following as brief examples to prompt group response
or select several to use to role play with the group.

"For example, a woman, who worked full time, had a
husband and grown children. She was the sibling desig-
nated by her family as responsible for the care of two
very sick parents who lived in their own home. She
was constantly berated and devalued by her mother, and
the mother was supported in this role by the father.
She was always the scapegoated child in the family, was
always trying to win the approval of her mother, without success. Even now, she provided much of their
cooked food, drives them to doctors' appointments, even
though her father still does some limited driving. She
has colitis and recalls that her daily phone

conversations with her parents are hurtful when mother still calls her 'messy, fat, and sloppy', berates her efforts in general and is never appreciative of what she does."

Role play the telephone call situation. Ask a group member to play the parent, the leader takes the adult-child role. Model expression of feelings by saying to mother, "When you call me names and say things that belittle me it hurts me very much and makes me feel bad. You may not be aware of this, but what you say to me can hurt me and make me feel very bad. I care very much for you Mom, but I sure wish you would let me know that you like me and approve of some of the things I've accomplished in my life. I'm a pretty nice person."

2. A woman was struggling with feelings about her father's remarriage, following her mother's painful and pro-tracted death. She was struggling to forgive her father for choosing another wife, and in some ways regarded his remarriage as a personal rejection of both herself and her mother.

In the role play situation, she was encouraged to invite her father and his new wife to dinner, to get to know the new wife, and to let her father know that she understood and approved his need to remarry.

3. A man was concerned that his college-aged children did not want to visit their grandmother when they were in the city. He felt torn between understanding his children's needs to spend their time as they chose, and in wanting them to accept some responsibility toward their grnadmother.

   In the role play it can be pointed out that the grand-children have a responsibility to spend time with their grandmother, but that they had the choice about when to visit.

4. Additional Suggestions for Role Plays
   If your group does not suggest materials for role plays, or you do not wish to elicit such material, here are some situations which we have utilized for successful role play:
   a. Parent insists that Aunt Belle be invited to your big party, when you had not planned to include her.
   b. Mother calls to tell you the night before you and your spouse are leaving for a long-planned vacation that she is sick and lonely and will miss you terribly and probably be in the hospital or dead when you return.
   c. Parent says to you that the neighbors in the apartment building are very mean and inconsiderate, and wants you to "tell them off."
   d. Parent calls you several times a day out of loneliness and boredom; and wants to know where you

were and what you were doing when you didn't answer,
and what you're fixing for supper.

e. Mother tells you that she is very worried about
    your father who seems to be disoriented most of
    the time, is soiling himself and forgetful, and
    she wants you to help her decide what to do.

f. Parent, who is a widow, tells you that she is be-
    coming frightened about living in her apartment
    and would like to know how you feel about her moving
    into that nice big room in your home that your
    married son has vacated.

g. Parent calls from a shopping center to say she's
    had a dizzy spell and doesn't know what to do.

III. VALUES CLARIFICATION EXERCISES

The exercises suggested here were chosen to reinforce the concept that we have needs and rights and if we have not been sufficiently loved or approved or validated by our parents, we can begin to validate and love ourselves in a healing fashion.[1] Depending upon time and style, you may choose a few or all of these exercises. The time that each exercise requires depends not so much upon the execution, but rather on the extent of the ensuing discussion.

A. Reality Time Pie
    1. Instructions

        Place a sample time pie on a flipchart or blackboard.

REALITY TIME PIE

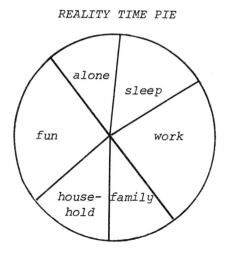

---

1. These exercises were adapted from Sid Simon, <u>Meeting Yourself Halfway</u> (Niles, Ill.: Argus Communications, 1974).

"On a sheet of paper, or on a 5" x 8" card, draw a
circle. Divide this circle to represent how you spend
your time in such categories as sleeping, working,
playing, and so on. You are free to use whatever
categories are important to you, and to determine
the amount of time spent. Because many activities
occur weekly rather than daily, we base this time
pie on a week's activities."

2. Discussion

Have each member share his or her time pie. The
device of sharing provides self-enhancement. Many may
be surprised at how they spend their time, and say
that this is a real eye-opener, others begin to
comment that some changes need to be made.

B. Fantasy Time Pie

1. Instructions

"On the back of the Reality Time Pie sheet, draw
another circle. This time divide the circle as you
would like it to be if you had free choice."

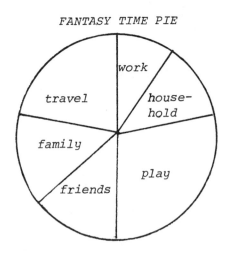

FANTASY TIME PIE

2. Discussion

The members enjoy doing this, and there may be much talking and laughing in the process. Usually there will be one member who has identical reality and fantasy time pies. The group may accept this as an "ideal" state, more sophisticated members may raise questions or even express some doubt about this and say there seems to be some denial. This exercise is particularly helpful as it encourages gratification and the expression of needs and wants.

C. Life Line Exercise

This exercise ties in nicely with the time pie exercises and puts one's life span into clearer perspective and focus.

birth date	marriage	birth of son	today's date	son's college grad.	world cruise	death date
10/5/45	6/20/63	7/2/70	1/4/80	1992	1993	12/31/2038

SAMPLE LIFE LINE

1. Instructions

Put a sample life line on the flipchart or blackboard. "On an 8-1/2" x 11" paper, draw a horizontal line lengthwise, in the middle of the paper. At the left

end put a dot and your birthdate. At the right end
put a dot and guesstimate your deathdate. Between
these two dots put a dot indicating today's date.
Between your birthdate and today's date, choose
significant events and dot and date them. These
dates may be anything at all. Between today's date
and your deathdate, place two dots, and date them,
indicating two significant events that you want to
happen between now and the time you die."

2. Discussion

Members have no difficulty with their birthdates but
are resistant and frightened about selecting a deathdate. This is a good place to talk about death and
fears of dying, relating it to how much more parents
must think about dying. Stress that we all die, we
need to begin to accept that as a fact and talking
about it is helpful. Merely doing this exercise
helps move the group closer to the concept of death
and its inevitability. It can be catharctic to talk
for a few minutes about the fears and fantasies of
what happens at death. Many members will acknowledge
that they have never allowed themselves to think of
their own death, this is like opening a door which
they have always kept closed. As the discussion
continues, you may hear responses such as, "I've never
thought I'd die until recently, and I had a hard time
accepting that until my father developed cancer.
Seeing him suffer has made me begin to think about
dying, his and mine. It's not easy to talk about
death over lunch, or at the dinner table."

Members usually choose as the significant dates between birth and today, such things as their marriage
date, or birth of a first child. Other choices have
included significant deaths, beginning a new job,
divorce date, becoming a grandmother, serious illness,
geographic move, moving into first home, and so on.

The responses between today's date and the death date
have included becoming a grandmother, being remarried,
losing weight, taking a world cruise, going back to
school, moving into a condominium from present large
home, retiring, beginning a second career, and so on.
This future prediction helps mobilize members to
consider options and choices which they have, and
points up how much control they do have in exercising
those options.

These simple exercises can be extremely effective and
members will refer to their reactions in the coming
sessions and will usually indicate that as a result
they are seriously considering changes and modifica-
tions in their lives.

D. Basic Needs Exercise

1. Instructions

"On another sheet of paper or index card, list your
five basic needs, in order of importance, the first
being the most important of your needs." Group
members may ask for clarification, do you mean food
and shelter?

"This is an exercise about which there will be no
direction as to content, in order not to lead or
influence your responses. Whatever you consider
your own five basic necessary needs are the appropriate response."

2. Discussion

Ask the group to read their lists in a quick go-
round. Doing this is self-enhancing and gratifying
to the members. The most frequently given need has
been to feel loved. If that has not been the first
choice, it is almost always included in the basic
five. Other sample responses are:

To feel wanted

To be able to care for others who need me

To like myself and feel good about myself, accept
myself as I am

To have privacy and time to be alone

To have friends and be included in social activities

To be a good mother, wife, daughter, sister,
daughter-in-law, sister-in-law, grandmother, friend,
worker

To do creative work

To have fun

To exercise (tennis, golf, swimming) and do the
things I like and enjoy without feeling guilty

To keep myself busy, well-informed, and involved
in life

To do meaningful work

To pursue my hobbies

Time to do nothing

To continue the learning process

To look attractive and keep my figure

IV. HOW TO BE A HAPPY AND SUCCESSFUL ADULT CHILD TO YOUR PARENT

A. Mini-lecture

"What we did today in the exercises and the discussion
following them was to focus on you and your rights and
needs. We attempted to move you toward a consideration
of who you are and what you want. Many of you acknowledged
that you had not given thought to what your rights or
needs were and that it was a new way of looking at yourself. I want to make a connection, or tie together the
concept of self-acceptance, including a legitimization of
needs and wants, with the way you relate to your parents.
These two seemingly separate concepts are interwoven and
must be understood as forming a pattern that will either
lead to a satisfying parental relationship, or one that
is nonsatisfying and painful. The extent of your happiness
and success as an adult child is based upon how you feel
about yourself.

"Let's go back and trace quickly how you learned to 'feel'
about yourself and judge and evaluate yourself. As
infants, we are totally dependent upon our parents or caretakers for our continued existence. We need to be fed,
changed, bathed, housed, fondled, cuddled, and taught. In
these early days we are very closely tied to our parents
and cannot exist without them. This is literally true;
infants cannot market, drive cars, write checks, or run
businesses. This early period of being totally dependent
on parents or caretakers is soon replaced by a period in

which young children begin to gain mastery over themselves and their environment as they learn to turn over, crawl, walk, talk, and feed themselves.

"As the child gains mastery, the parent has a part to play. The parents, who may have been gratified at having the baby dependent on them, must now give up their total control and care and encourage the young child to separate from them, to take risks, to make mistakes and to learn from them. One of the most difficult tasks of parenthood is to recognize when to separate and begin to let go. Parents who are constantly vigilant, over-protective, watchful beyond what is reasonable, or who are totally non-involved, may give messages to their children that the child is not okay, or capable of being loved or able to take care of him or herself. This is failing to validate the young child. It means that the parents haven't encouraged the child to do things for him or herself, or haven't allowed the child to take reasonable risks and learn from their mistakes. Parents who allow and encourage this to happen, providing proper love and guidance, are really <u>validating</u> their children, saying without words, that they are okay and can take care of themselves, and we respect and love you.

"By validating children, parents say that they love their children unconditionally, or just as they are. Such children can usually feel good about themselves, and accept themselves and be helpful to others.

"Unvalidated children may become unvalidated adults. These adults may be sad, depressed, angry or guilty in a vague way, feeling that they didn't quite measure up to their parents' expectations. As adult children they may find that assuming responsibility for their aging parents is enormously difficult because they haven't worked out the earlier relationship and are still seeking their parents' approval and love.

"What can you do if your parents have not validated you? First of all, for the most part your parents did the best job they could in parenting you. They were someone's children too, and perhaps didn't receive all that they needed. Second, you can validate yourself, and much of what we have been talking about involves just that--coming to terms with who you are, what you need, recognizing that you have to be yourself, and that you are an acceptable human being. You must work toward accepting yourself unconditionally. If there are parts of you that you believe are unacceptable, you have the potential to change and modify them.

"Now, how can we be happy and successful adult children to our parents? Clearly, there is no magic formula. But, beyond what we've stressed as basic self-acceptance there are ways of relating to parents which can ease difficult relationships and improve good relationships.

"It is important that in whatever way we help our parents as they become more dependent on us, the manner in which we

help them is critical. Many of you have sick or disoriented or healthy but 'trying' parents. You may feel
harrassed, overburdened, and plain angry. Your feelings
show! Help your parents as much as possible with as much
good humor and grace as possible. It helps to remember
that you are going to be old, too, some day, and will
want your children to treat you kindly.

"Respect the dignity of your parents, particularly as they
age and may lose ground. Help without undermining your
parents' independence as much as possible. If you find
resources that your parents can use, put them in touch
with them, but don't consider this as a substitute for your
self or what you personally can provide. If you can
sincerely do so, let your parents know that you love
them, care for them, and that they can depend on you when
they need you. Let them know that you will not make plans
for them, but with them. Talk to them so that you know
what their wishes are if a time should come when you need
to be in charge and make decisions for them.

"Relate to your parents in a loving spirit. When you can
do so sincerely, remember to smile at, touch, stroke, hug,
kiss and embrace your parents. Older people especially are
very much in need of physical contact.

"As people age, they may feel less attractive and less
lovable, therefore, it's very important that you make
physical contact as appropriate. Studies have shown that
infants in a nursery who were not picked up, handled and

fondled, wasted and failed to thrive. Some of these children, although well fed, died as a result of little or no
physical contact.[2] It may be difficult if you are not
demonstrative by nature to suddenly begin making physical
contact with your parents. Do only what is comfortable
for you. Simply touching your parent's back, stroking an
arm, or holding a hand can be very loving and meaningful.
A warm smile and a hug can mean a great deal.

"Maintain regular contact, by telephone and in person, based
on your lifestyle and preference. Be certain to include
your parents in family and holiday celebrations. Have
them to your home and visit them where they live. It's
also nice to plan outings with your parents, appropriate to
their health and interests.

"When you buy gifts for your parents, be imaginative.
Instead of bedroom slippers, dietetic candy, or a heating
pad, what about a bird in a gilded cage, season's tickets
to the theater or opera, a gift certificate for a new
hairdo, facial, make-up session, manicure, or pedicure,
a dinner prepared by you for your parents and their friends,
a cassette recorder for precious reminiscences of early
memories, or an easel and paints for creative hobbying?

---

2. René A. Spitz, "Hospitalism: An Inquiry into the Genesis of
Psychiatric Conditions in Early Childhood," in The Psychoanalytic
Study of the Child, vol. 1, ed. Otto Fenichel et al. (New York:
International Universities Press, 1945), pp. 53-74.

"Encourage your parents to take an active part in the community in which they live. This may not be an option for parents who are seriously ill or debilitated. Bring as much of the community to them as possible, news of the outside, books, magazines, newspapers, photos and people from the outside. Older persons need stimulation, particularly if they are in a hospital or nursing home.

"Finish any unfinished business with your parents, don't wait until they've died to say 'I'm sorry', or to help them say 'I'm sorry' to you. Talk honestly about feelings, and about concerns. If your parents want to talk about their dying, you can be helpful and supportive and reassuring by talking and listening.

"Always treat your parents as adults. Respect their strengths and weaknesses. Forgive their past mistakes and accept them as human beings who happen to be your parents."

B. Discussion

This mini-lecture is designed to stimulate, encourage and give "permission" to these adult children to rethink and reconsider their old relationship with parents and move into a relationship of filial maturity.

Members may respond to the concepts, suggestions, and ideas in the mini-lecture and "try-them-on-for-size," with the support of the group. Old resentments die hard, but they can be dealt with and diminished.

V. HOME ASSIGNMENT

Ask group members who do not wear glasses to bring either a pair
of sunglasses, or someone else's glasses for next week's session.
Do not explain why you want the glasses. Send a note to that
effect to absent members.

HANDOUTS

FOR

SESSION 3

HOW TO BE A HAPPY AND SUCCESSFUL ADULT CHILD TO YOUR PARENTS

If you feel that your parent has not accepted you or loved you or validated you sufficiently, stop trying to make it happen, but begin to find new ways of accepting yourself, loving yourself and validating yourself as a human being.

Remember that your parents probably did as good a job of parenting you as they had capacity for. They were someone's children once, too!

Remember that your parents have needs and rights.

Help your parents as needed, with good humor and grace.

Help without undermining independence. Respect your parent's dignity.

When you suggest available resources to your parents, do not consider this as a substitute for yourself or what you can do.

Do not plan for, but with your parents for their care, as long as they can reasonably be involved in the planning. Become aware of their wishes and desires now, so that you can respond accordingly if you should have to make decisions for them at a later time.

Let your parents know that you love them, that you admire and respect them (if you do) and let them know in a loving spirit that you will be there when they need you.

Be physically involved by smiling at, touching, stroking, hugging, kissing, and embracing (but not if it is completely alien to you) your parents.

Maintain regular phone and personal contact.

Invite your parents to your home, and visit your parents where they live. Include your parents in family and holiday celebrations and plan outings appropriate to your parents' interests and health. Provide ample opportunity for your parents to be with you, your children, and your grandchildren.

Bring the outside world to your parent who is ill or debilitated. If your parent is physically isolated through illness, she or he needs as much stimulation as you can provide with books, magazines, conversations and friend's visits.

Be imaginative in the gifts you buy and do remember anniversary occasions.

Finish any unfinished business with your parents, say "I'm sorry" and help them to say "I'm sorry" to you.

If your parent wants to discuss death, either imminent or distant, listen and respond as honestly and realistically as possible. Assure your parent that you will carry out any wishes regarding funeral arrangements and so on.

Treat your parents as adults; accept them as human beings who happen to be your parents.

Maintain a sense of humor!

MY DECLARATION OF SELF-ESTEEM[3]

I am me.

In all the world, there is no one else exactly like me. There are persons who have some parts like me, but no one adds up exactly like me. Therefore, everything that comes out of me is authentically mine because I alone chose it.

I own everything about me--my body, including everything it does; my mind, including all its thoughts and ideas; my eyes, including the images of all they behold; my feelings, whatever they may be-- anger, joy, frustrations, love, disappointment, excitement; my mouth and all words that come out of it, polite, sweet or rough, correct or incorrect; my voice, loud or soft; and all my actions, whether they be to others or to myself.

I own my fantasies, my dreams, my hopes, my fears.

I own all my triumphs and successes, all my failures and mistakes.

Because I own all of me, I can become intimately acquainted with me. By so doing I can love me and be friendly with me in all my parts. I can then make it possible for all of me to work in my best interests.

---

3. Virginia Satir, Peoplemaking (Palo Alto, Calif.: Science and Behavior Books, 1972), pp. 27-29. Reprinted with permission.

I know there are aspects about myself that puzzle me, and other aspects that I do not know. But as long as I am friendly and loving to myself, I can courageously and hopefully look for the solutions to the puzzles and for ways to find out more about me.

However I look and sound, whatever I say and do, and whatever I think and feel at a given moment in time is me. This is authentic and represents where I am at that moment in time.

When I review later how I looked and sounded, what I said and did, and how I thought and felt, some parts may turn out to be unfitting. I can discard that which is unfitting, and keep that which proved fitting, and invent something new for that which I discarded.

I can see, hear, feel, think, say, and do. I have the tools to survive, to be close to others, to be productive, and to make sense and order out of the world of people and things outside of me.

I own me, and therefore I can engineer me.

I am me and I am okay.

SESSION 4

SESSION 4

BRIEF OUTLINE

OBJECTIVE: To sensitize the group to the experience of aging.

PREPARATION

    A. Setting the Stage
    B. Materials Required
    C. Time Allottment

  I. WELCOME AND UPDATE

 II. VALUES CLARIFICATION EXERCISES

    A. Glasses and Earplugs
    B. Old People Are . . .
    C. Discussion

III. THE AGING PROCESS: PHYSICAL AND EMOTIONAL ASPECTS

    A. Mini-lecture
    B. Discussion

 IV. HANDOUTS

SESSION 4

PREPARATION

A. <u>Setting the Stage</u>
   1. Lower the lights and/or darken the room.
   2. Provide background noise, a radio or tape.

B. <u>Materials Needed</u>
   1. Vaseline to smear the eyeglasses
   2. Cotton balls to use as earplugs
   3. Paper and pencils
   4. Facial tissue to clean the eyeglasses (or use glass cleaner)
   5. A few pairs of glasses for group members who forget
   6. Prepare handouts

C. <u>Time Allotment</u>
   I.   Welcome and Update   10 minutes
   II. Values Clarification Exercises   35 minutes
   III. Mini-lecture and Discussion   35 minutes
   IV. Handout   <u>10 minutes</u>
                                              90 minutes

SESSION 4

I. WELCOME AND UPDATE

This is the time to tell the group that you are halfway through
the workshop. You may be asked to consider extending the workshop, or provide a "second series." Consider the options and
plan to discuss the alternatives with the group at the last
session. It is important to be aware that to continue this group
might be a move toward a therapy group. Or, suggest that members
consider joining other available workshops, or a new workshop on
a different but related subject.

The group will do an update on their own progress and share
reports on their parents. You will hear positive as well as
negative reports, but may notice that the members have internal-
ized a great deal of the workshop material and are changing and
modifying behavior and utilizing new approaches and new coping
methods. The group is aware of this and as they discuss these
changes, they can make positive comments about what they are
doing. Members who had only spoken in a negative way about a
parent will now begin to view the parent in a more sympathetic
light and talk about understanding why the parent is feeling
grumpy or sad or needy.

II. VALUES CLARIFICATION EXERCISES

A. Glasses and Earplugs

You must maintain an attitude of annoyance with the group, and speak so softly that you are not easily understood. As group members ask you to speak more loudly, do so by raising your voice inappropriately and expressing your displeasure at being asked to repeat.

The group will struggle with this exercise and mutter and grumble. The more they complain, the more successful you have been in carrying out this exercise. Take as much time as needed. This is an impressive exercise and you can do much to facilitate the process and give the group a feeling of being unfairly and insensitively treated. This is an exercise which will be long remembered. The questions asked are very difficult for almost anyone to know without some digging. Let it be known that the group is somehow "deficient," "slow," or "stupid" if they do not have the correct answers.

1. Collect the eyeglasses each member in the group was asked to bring. Liberally smear the lenses with vaseline. Each group member must wear the glasses to do this exercise.

2. Distribute cotton balls and instruct the group to plug their ears.

3. Turn up the "noise" on the radio, lower your voice and speak softly to increase the difficulty of being heard. Group members may not want to wear the glasses at first because they severely diminish visual acuity. Insist

that they wear the glasses.

4. Tell the group to "Take out your notebooks and write the following."

The group will respond with, "What notebooks? You forgot to tell us to bring notebooks."

Respond in harsh tone, "You always forget what you're told. I will have to give paper to you."

Distribute paper but no pen or pencil. Some members will have a pen or pencil . . . others may ask, "Where are the pens today?"

Respond, again harshly, "Can't you take care of things for yourself, you'd think you would have enough sense by now to carry a pen." Express annoyance by facial expression (pained, bored), looking at your watch, tapping on the table and toe-tapping. Put your hand to your head and sigh a lot. Do not smile.

5. Ask the group to write the following on the paper provided.

Speak softly.
1. Your social security number
2. Your automobile license number
3. Your grandmother's maiden name, date, and place of her birth
4. The names of your kindergarten and first grade teacher

5. The exact amount of money you have in your purse or wallet

6. The location of your birth certificate, marriage certificate and insurance policies

7. Your blood type

6. Turn up the lights, turn off the "noise," smile, distribute the facial tissue to clean the glasses and have the group remove the earplugs.

7. Discussion

Ask for reactions. You will have a hard time keeping everyone from answering at once. For example, the group felt:

Angry

Frustrated

Unfairly treated

Slow

Stupid

Like a child

Helpless

Like crying or leaving

Like refusing to do anything

Physically sick

Wanted to be back at home where it was safe

Out of control

Defenseless

Discussion will be lively as the group shares their feelings. Direct the discussion toward how it would be to feel this way permanently--without being able to wipe the "cataracts" away with a facial tissue or restore hearing by removing a cotton ball. Focus

discussion on being sensitive to what it feels like to
be treated harshly, unfairly, without kindness or
empathy, and only because one is experiencing sensory
deprivation not of one's choice!

B. Old People Are . . .

You will need two copies of the form "Old People Are . . ."
(see Handout Section page 117) for each group member.
1. Distribute the form and ask the group to complete it
   and turn it face side down.
2. Distribute a second copy of the same form. Tell the
   group to imagine themselves to be 75 years old, and
   to complete the form as they would respond at that age.

C. Discussion

These exercises should provide and stimulate much thoughtful
discussion. Move the group toward feeling, understanding,
and empathizing with what their parents are experiencing,
but without moralizing, valuing, or being judgmental. The
group may note that the "Old People Are . . ." forms filled
out the first time were critical and negative, but that the
forms filled out the second time were more positive and
less harsh.
Summarize broadly as follows:
1. Aging brings changes
2. Your parents are aging
3. You will age too
4. Planning for later years can be full, rich and gratifying
5. As you are now, so you will be in later life, but
   more so!

III. THE AGING PROCESS: PHYSICAL AND EMOTIONAL ASPECTS

A. Mini-lecture

"Today, in a purposefully dramatic way, you had an opportunity to glimpse for a fraction of a second a revocable experience in aging. You may have felt frustrated, helpless, angry, out of control and you didn't like what was happening to you!

"You wanted the exercise to end. You wanted to be able to see, hear, and function as you normally do, without being harrassed or hassled by anyone telling you what to do and how to do it, and furthermore how ineffectively you were doing it.

"Magnify this experience, imagine that it is not revocable, that it is not going to be reversed, and perhaps it may get worse. I am painting a negative picture not because I believe aging is necessarily negative, but because what actually happens to many people as they grow older is negative and devastating. Part of what happens has to do with how we treat our elderly, based on our own lack of understanding and sensitivity and also our own fear of aging and death which makes us distance ourselves from any evidence of growing old.

"Aging brings changes in many ways. Aging and growing old can be an extremely rich period, a time for growth, maturation, renewal, and preparation for one's ending. We will be looking at the physical and emotional aspects of aging in a broad sense. Some of the more obvious changes which occur emphasize that aging does indeed bring a multitude of both observable and subtle changes.

"What are some of the physical changes in aging? Aging itself is a lifelong process. It is also an imprecise term because it has so many different meanings, and there are many separate concepts of old age. Some forms of illness are found more often in people past middle age. On the other hand, many people live to their eighties and nineties entirely or reasonably healthy. Aging often brings some degree of sensory loss for most people. Some older people develop loss of sharp vision.

"For the elderly who experience an appreciable loss of vision, it may mean an end to a lifelong pleasure in reading books. It may also mean an end to reading a daily newspaper and a subsequent out-of-touch feeling regarding world events and local news. Loss of vision may mean an inability to continue valued correspondence with loved ones and an inability to write checks to pay bills. It may interfere with driving a car, using a bus, watching television, marketing, and getting around town. It may mean refusing to step outside the walls of a 'safe' apartment or home in which the elderly can feel her way around the rooms with minimal risk of bumping into furniture or walls. Loss of visual acuity may mean a discontinuation of hobbies such as needlework, painting, cooking, playing cards or playing tennis and golf.

"Many elderly may also experience a loss in hearing. Most people beyond the age of fifty cannot hear high frequencies. This is not a major problem because the frequency of human speech is well below that level. However, disease may result in even frequencies in the lower levels being difficult to hear. People who do not hear well may become socially isolated, feel leftout, shunned, and embarrassed by their loss.

"Digestion may become a problem because of the loss of teeth or poorly fitting dentures. As we age, our bones lose calcium and become brittle. Older bones are more prone to fracture and also less amenable to healing. Joints may become inflamed and arthritis and rheumatism are frequent and painful problems for the elderly. As a result, older people may become extremely cautious about climbing stairs and venturing out of doors in wet, snowy or icy weather.

"As we age, our appearance begins to change. Strength is diminished and there may be a generalized loss of vigor. Skin may begin to wrinkle and sag. Muscles lose their elasticity and clothes may not fit as well as they once did. Voices may become thin and reedy, and hands become gnarled. Older people may lose all or most of their teeth or have other dental problems which require extensive and expensive correction. Older people may be quite embarrassed about wearing dentures and occasionally have so much difficulty chewing that they refuse dinner invitations. Noses grow longer, and there is hair thinning and hair loss, both on the head and on the body. Veins and pores enlarge and eyes may become rheumy. In very advanced years the mouth may remain agape and the spinal column may become curved. Older people actually shrink.

"In men, the prostate gland enlarges and creates a need for frequent urination. In women, voluptuous curves disappear, the breasts sag, the vaginal walls lose much of their lubricating secretions and the problem of brittle bones, or osteoporosis is seen more frequently.

"Sexually, both men and women may remain active into their eighties and beyond, although there is less frequency.

"As we age, diseases such as diabetes, high blood pressure, and hiatal hernia are common. These diseases are not necessarily life threatening, but represent a frightening change in lifestyle. Circulation may be sluggish causing pains after walking short distances. Poor circulation may create other physical problems of a more serious nature. These may be heart problems, or major strokes with some subsequent impairment. Sometimes memory may be faulty or thought process may become disordered. Tempers may flare as insults are felt (either real or imagined).

"Aging brings changes in sleeping patterns. The elderly may have difficulty sleeping the night through, although there is an increased tendency to doze or nap during the day.

"For the elderly, there is a higher incidence of accidents in the home. As strength diminishes, routine tasks once easily accomplished may become dangerous and frightening. Using the stove may be hazardous for those who do not see well, or are not strong enough to lift heavy pots. Getting into and out of the bathtub may be a frightening experience and many older women have great difficulty washing their own hair.

"To sum up, although in some cases the physical process of aging may be slight or negligible, it may affect your parents in very severe or disabling manner. Heredity, general outlook on life, fate and finances have much to do with how one ages.

"You must also consider the emotional aspects of aging. Generally, aging exaggerates earlier personality characteristics. If your parents were always cheerful and optimistic they will probably continue to be so. If your parents were always sour and acerbic, they will probably continue to be so. Some emotional changes, however, may result from disease or neurological trauma.

"Even in the absence of a major physical disease, your parents will be faced with the loss of family members and lifetime friends and may become increasingly lonely. As your parents move into their eighties and nineties they will experience more and more losses. Older people pay a great deal of attention to the obituary column and keep score of "who's left."

"As your parents' contemporaries die, they are left with
fewer and fewer people who knew them in their prime; young,
strong, capable, and attractive. With those old friends
and family members they did not have to prove anything.
It is a difficult task for most older people to let a
'new' friend know the full flavor of what she or he has
been, and what she or he has accomplished in her lifetime.

"One of the most emotionally devastating experiences of
life is losing a spouse. If this has happened to your
parent, she or he may still be mourning and grieving this
loss. As your parents age, lose a mate, or other family
members and friends, they may feel increasingly lonely for
someone who loved them well and knew and admired them.
Your parents may struggle against the loss of independence,
may have less income, fewer decisions of any consequence
to make, and feel less needed. There are fewer oppor-
tunities as individuals reach their eighties and nineties
to begin a second career, although there are notable
exceptions to this. If parents are widowed it may
necessitate a move from the home where precious memories
were built. For older people moving usually means to a
smaller place and involves giving up many cherished
possessions.

"There is a preoccupation in aging with death and illness.
Older persons have a realistic concern about the boundaries
of pain to be tolerated in illness, with feared loss of
control and dignity. Parents who have been very active
in their early and mid years may find that they cannot

function without the structure of work or busy homelife, and it may be too late to learn new skills if this has not been started in the mid years.

"Parents may become less flexible as they age, become less willing to try new things. For any number of reasons, parents may be unreasonable and hard to talk to. They may simply be grieving or frightened or both. Older people are not always treated with kindness or considera- tion or respect. They are often times demeaned and de- valued, and have few ways of coping or fighting back. One way is what we call the life review:

> The tendency of the elderly toward self-reflection
> and reminiscence used to be thought of as indi-
> cating a loss of recent memory and therefore a
> sign of aging. However, in 1961 one of us (R.N.B.)
> postulated that reminiscence in the aged was part
> of a normal life review process brought about by
> realization of approaching dissolution and death.
> It is characterized by the progressive return to
> consciousness of past experiences and particularly
> the resurgence of unresolved conflicts which can
> be looked at again and reintegrated. If the re-
> integration is successful, it can give new sig-
> nificance and meaning to one's life and prepare
> one for death, by mitigating fear and anxiety.
>
> This is a process that is believed to occur
> universally in all persons in the final years
> of their lives, although they may not be totally
> aware of it and may in part defend themselves
> from realizing its presence. It is spontaneous,
> unselective, and seen in other age groups as
> well (adolescence, middle age); but the intensity
> and emphasis on putting one's life in order are
> most striking in old age. In late life people
> have a particularly vivid imagination and memory

for the past and can recall with sudden and
remarkable clarity early life events. There
is renewed ability to free-associate and
bring up material from the unconscious.
Individuals realize that their own personal
myth of invulnerability and immortality can
no longer be maintained. All of this results
in reassessment of life, which brings depression, acceptance, or satisfaction.

The life review can occur in mild form through
mild nostalgia, mild regret, a tendency to
reminisce, story-telling, and the like. Often
the person will give his life story to anyone
who will listen. At other times it is con-
ducted in monologue without another person
hearing it. It is in many ways similar to
the psychotherapeutic situation in which a
person is reviewing his life in order to
understand his present circumstances.

As part of the life review one may experience
a sense of regret that is increasingly painful. In severe forms it can yield anxiety,
guilt, despair, and depression. And in
extreme cases if a person is unable to
resolve problems or accept them, terror,
panic, and suicide can result. The most
tragic life review is that in which a person
decides life was a total waste.

Some of the positive results of reviewing
one's life can be a righting of old wrongs,
making up with enemies, coming to acceptance
of mortal life, a sense of serenity, pride
in accomplishment, and a feeling of having
done one's best. It gives people an opportunity to decide what to do with the time
left to them and work out emotional and
material legacies. People become ready
but in no hurry to die. Possibly the
qualities of serenity, philosophical development, and wisdom observable in some older
people reflect a state of resolution of their

life conflicts. A lively capacity to live in
the present is usually associated, including
the direct enjoyment of elemental pleasures
such as nature, children, forms, colors,
warmth, love, and humor. One may become
more capable of mutuality with a comfortable
acceptance of the life cycle, the universe,
and the generations. Creative works may
result such as memoirs, art, and music.
People may put together family albums and
scrapbooks and study their genealogies.
[The Smithsonian Institution is gathering
such memorabilia and reminiscences from
individuals and families for its two-year
Bicentennial education program entitled
"Your own American Experience." For
information on how to participate, write
Kin and Communities Program, The Smithsonian
Institution, Washington, D.C. 20560.]

One of the greatest difficulties for younger
persons (including mental health personnel)
is to listen thoughtfully to the reminiscences
of older people. . . . We have been taught
that this nostalgia represents living in the
past and a preoccupation with self and
that it is generally boring, meaningless,
and time-consuming. Yet as a natural healing
process it represents one of the underlying
human capacities on which all psychotherapy
depends. The life review as a necessary and
healthy process should be recognized in
daily life as well as used in mental health
care of older people.[1]

"All in all, in looking at the physical and emotional

aspects of the aging process, it can be concluded that

---

1. Reproduced with permission from Robert N. Butler and Myrna I.
Lewis, Aging and Mental Health, 2 ed., 1977 (St. Louis: C. V.
Mosby, 1977), pp. 49-50.

although it may not be particularly difficult or troubled, your parents may experience one or several of the problems described. Even if your parents enjoy robust health, and are emotionally healthy, they will experience some slowing down and will suffer some losses. Your parents will be needing all of the love and support and understanding which you are able to provide.

"In particular, your parents will need strength and integrity to face their old age, aging, and death."

B. Discussion

Acknowledge the sense of sadness as the group members share feelings for the "parent that was." You will hear statements of compassion and increasing empathy and sensitivity to a realization of what some of the parents are experiencing. For others whose parents are in good health there is very real sense of relief, mixed with a heightened sense of what may come.

Members talk about a new awareness of their parents' real loneliness and fears as family and friends die. The group can understand the importance of trigenerational interchange and the value of this coming together for all members of the family, but also recognize that this is not a substitute for one's peers.

There are usually some expressions that show compassion for parents who are "loners." Members have expressed understanding that they can see how difficult it would be for parents who never did much socializing to now begin going to community centers and senior citizen groups. Often times this subject has been a sore spot between an anxious adult child and parent. Adult children sometimes become insistent that parents who have previously operated within a very limited social sphere now, deprived of a spouse, begin to seek out new friends and become active in "clubs."

Acknowledge the feeling tone of the discussion.

IV. HANDOUTS

Spend a few minutes reading the quotes "Quotations on Old Age" with the group. These are "up" quotes and are planned as an appropriate antidote to the material on the aging process.

HANDOUTS

FOR

SESSION 4

OLD PEOPLE ARE . . .

1. Old people should _____
_____
_____

2. Old people always _____
_____
_____

3. Old people look _____
_____
_____

4. Spending time with old people is _____
_____
_____

5. Old people need _____
_____
_____

6. Old people have rights to _____
_____
_____

7. As far as sex goes, old people _____
_____
_____

8. Old people can expect _____

    _____

    _____

9. Old people have power to _____

    _____

    _____

10. Old people's small fixed incomes are _____

    _____

    _____

QUOTATIONS ON OLD AGE

"To me, old age is always fifteen years older than I am." Bernard Baruch

"We ought not to heap reproaches on old age, seeing that we all hope to reach it." Bion

"Grow old along with me! The best is yet to be,
The last of life, for which the first was made."   Robert Browning

"We do not count a man's years until he has nothing else to count." Emerson

"As we grow old . . . the beauty stills inward." Emerson

"The sad wisdom of age wells up without sound." Sarah Teasdale

"There are people who are beautiful in dilapidation, like old houses that were hideous when new." Logan Pearsall Smith

"We must not take the faults of our youth into our old age, for old age brings with it its own defects." Goethe

"When grace is joined with wrinkles, it is adorable. There is an unspeakable dawn in happy old age." Victor Hugo

"Age is opportunity no less, than youth itself, though in another dress, and as the evening twilight fades away, the sky is filled with stars, invisible by day." Longfellow

"Growing old is no more than a bad habit that a busy man has not time to form." Andre Maurais

"You shall rise in the presence of grey hairs, give honour to the aged, and fear your God." Leviticus, XIX, 32

"Grey hair is a crown of glory, and it is won by a virtuous life." Proverbs, XVI, 31

"Honor your father and your mother, that you may live long in the land which the lord your God is giving you." Exodus XX, 12

SESSION 5

SESSION 5

BRIEF OUTLINE

OBJECTIVE: To acquaint the group with all of the available community resources which can be utilized in providing a network of support services for their parents.

PREPARATION

   A. Setting the Stage
   B. Materials Needed
   C. Time Allotment

I. WELCOME AND UPDATE

II. COMMUNITY RESOURCES

   A. Distribution of individual packets
   B. Discussion

III. EXERCISE--TWELVE CHARACTERISTICS

   A. Instructions
   B. Discussion

IV. WHEN IS IT TIME TO CONSIDER A CHANGE IN YOUR PARENTS'
LIVING ARRANGEMENTS OR LIFESTYLE?

    A. Mini-lecture
    B. Discussion

V. HOMEWORK ASSIGNMENT

HANDOUTS

SESSION 5

PREPARATION

A. <u>Setting the Stage</u>

The accumulation of community resource material may require a
period of several weeks in which various leaflets, brochures,
and pamphlets are mailed or delivered to you. Begin calling
agencies and resources in the first week of each workshop. Call
them again during the third week if you have not yet received
the material. Distributing this material during the fifth session
allows enough time to gather almost all of the material requested.

Ask for enough copies of material from each resource to provide
an individual copy for each member. Many members may be unaware
of the resources.

This is a checklist of places and agencies to contact for
material:

1. Social Security Office
   a. Social security benefits for persons 65 and over
   b. Medicare
   c. Medicaid
2. Public Welfare Office, for information on food stamps
3. Meals-on-Wheels programs which may be offered through churches
   or synagogues or community centers
4. Area Agency on Aging, a government sponsored group
5. Home-Helper Services available through local hospitals to
   recently discharged patients

6. Homemaker Services available through family service agencies and private organizations
7. Services to the Blind
8. Visiting Nurses Association Services
9. The Mayor's Committee on Aging has a multitude of programs and services
10. Internal Revenue Services, for tax relief for elderly home owners and renters
11. Protection against crime
12. Day care programs for older adults
13. Friendly Visiting Programs
14. Telephone Reassurance Programs
15. Counseling services
16. Low cost drugs for older adults
17. Free medical screening tests
18. Recreation for seniors at reduced rates
19. Consumer's guide for your state's nursing homes
20. Your state's Senior Citizens Handbook
21. Employment services for those over 65
22. Special services of the Cancer, Heart, and Diabetes Associations
23. Transportation services for elderly

As you go through the checklist you will uncover additional resources. Your community will probably have its own specialized programs and services for the elderly.

These packets will be large; put the material into a heavy-duty envelope which measures abour 14 x 10 inches. This package, which represents something "concrete," provides a great deal of support to the members.

Prepare copies of the exercise "Twelve Characteristics" for each member. A copy of this exercise is on page 143 of this session.

B. Materials Needed
   1. 8-1/2 x 11 inch paper
   2. Pens and Pencils

C. Time Allotment

I.	Welcome and Update	8 minutes
II.	Community Resources	30 minutes
III.	Exercise: "Twelve Characteristics"	20 minutes
IV.	Mini-lecture	30 minutes
V.	Handout and Homework Assignment	2 minutes
		90 minutes

SESSION 5

I. WELCOME AND UPDATE

Remind the group that there is one more session after today and say that at that time you will talk about their request to continue. The last session will be a wrap-up of what has been covered and learned, there will be a homework assignment for Session Six, we will put up the Goals Chart from the first session, and we will be completing a written brief evaluation of the workshop.

Members will spend time talking about their parents, but will probably spend more time talking about themselves and their changes and new insights. It is important to allow enough time for this. You may hear that the members are feeling better about themselves and about their parents. They relate that the parents are saying positive things to them and that there is less fighting. Members are having more regular and enjoyable contact with their siblings. There may be greater contact with the parents, which is enjoyable to members and parents, and a physical closeness which members have begun to initiate . . . touching, kissing, stroking. Apparently this is an overlooked area in many adult child-parent relationships and when approached in a loving spirit, brings joy to both.

II. COMMUNITY RESOURCES

A. <u>Distribution of Individual Packets of Materials</u>
Distribute the packet of materials you have collected to
each member. See instructions on collecting packet materials on page 125.

B. <u>Discussion of Each Resource</u>
Go through each piece of material and highlight the
important points in each. Spend as much time as necessary
explaining just what is available and who is eligible for
each service.

You may also choose to include your agency's brochure and
discuss agency services at this time rather than at the
first session. Or, you may repeat the information because
it will have more significance now.

Stress that it is best to use <u>all</u> possible combinations of
family, surrogate family, paid helpers, volunteer, and
community resources in a network of support services
before considering a move to a residential or nursing home
facility. The philosophy in the workshop is that as long
as your parent <u>wants</u> to remain in her own home and it is
reasonable and safe for her to do so this is indeed the
best plan.

129

III. EXERCISE "TWELVE CHARACTERISTICS"

A. Instructions

Distribute a copy of the exercise (see Handout Section page 143) and pens or pencils to each member.

"There are twelve characteristics and twelve numbered blank spaces. Arrange the characteristics according to their priority, the most important being number one and the least important number twelve."

Allow enough time for the group to make a final decision about the ordering of the characteristics.

B. Discussion

As the group discusses this exercise they will begin to make some judgments and comments as to how they view their parents.

If your group is small enough, doing a go-round in which each member shares their prioritized list, and tells why the choice was made is a good way for the group members to take a look at how they feel about their parents, what they really want from them and then to consider some good and positive factors about their parents.

The following questions can be used to facilitate discussion.

1. How can we encourage our parents to develop interests and hobbies and not be totally dependent upon us for social activities?

2. How can we "help" our parents not to intrude on our friends?

    a. Some parents call adult child's friends when the adult child cannot be reached by phone.

    b. Some parents are extremely critical of the adult-child's friends and criticize them constantly.

    c. Some parents ask the adult child's friends to run errands for them or perform other chores. This is often embarrassing to the adult child, who then feels "negligent" and "guilty."

3. How can we avoid treating our parents like children?

If time allows, role play one or two situations presented.

IV. WHEN IS IT TIME TO CONSIDER A CHANGE IN YOUR PARENTS' LIVING ARRANGEMENTS OR LIFESTYLE?

A. Mini-lecture

"One of the most difficult decisions which you will ever be called on to make, is planning a change in your parents' living arrangements or lifestyle. Some of you have already experienced this situation, some are at the point of making such a decision, some are years away from such decision making, and some will never need to do this. But for all of you, at whatever stage you are, and whatever you have experienced, the overwhelming feelings which usually accompany this decision making are ones of sadness, soberness, unhappiness, and guilt. We really want and need to be certain that we have made the right decision for our parents. To make certain that our decision is wise, we need to include parents, family, and doctors in the decision and plan making. The final decision then becomes the result of thoughtful and shared responsibility.

"Before any final decision is considered, there are some signs or clues that can be used as a guide to determine whether any change needs to be made. Certain signposts indicate when some extra help or change in living is necessary. These clues or signs are the danger signals.

"If one or two of the danger signals are present, it is probably not significant. If, however, several are present, it is probably time to consider a change.

132

"When we talk about a change in living arrangements there are several options, and do not all necessarily mean a nursing or residential home. It may be entirely possible to maintain your parent in her or his own home with an appropriate support system. Or a move to a smaller apartment, an efficiency perhaps, or a move from a large home to a more manageable apartment might be considered. Consider as many options and alternatives as possible.

"The danger signals are:

"Sudden weight loss. You notice that your parent is losing weight suddenly, as a result of not eating or not preparing food. This occurs frequently as a parent loses visual acuity and is afraid to use the stove. If your parent is weak and cooking becomes an effort, or marketing is too difficult, food preparation may decrease. A man who has been widowed, who is unaccustomed to taking care of himself, let alone cooking for himself, may lose weight. Any weight loss needs to be investigated medically. Remedies may be Meals-on-Wheels, bringing in prepared meals several times a week, or hiring a housekeeper or neighbor to do the marketing and meal preparation. An apartment with a dining room for residents may be another choice or a 'roommate' or 'boarder' who would prepare meals, do marketing, and clean-up. Discuss the choices with your parent and family and come to a decision after considering all the options.

"Failure to take medication or overtaking medication. You may become aware, for instance, that your parent is failing to take medication as needed. One man wanted to eat more than he was allowed on his diabetic regime, and so without the doctor's approval, he increased his dosage of insulin, with very serious consequences. Be alert for this and consider it a sign that some help is needed.

"Burn marks or injury marks. These marks may be an indication of physical problems involving general weakness, or may be an indication of forgetfulness. The parent who has burnmarks on hands, fingers, and arms, as well as on clothing, or bruise marks on face and body may be forgetting to put out matches and cigarettes, or may be having blackouts with subsequent falls and bruising.

"Deterioration of personal habits. You may notice that your usually well-groomed and immaculate parent is bathing infrequently, is not shaving his face, washing her hair as needed, or is failing to wear dentures. There may be a disinterest in using grooming and cosmetic aids. Clothing may go unchanged for days or weeks at a time.

"Increasing car accidents of a minor or major nature. This may be an indication of slowed reflexes, poor vision, physical weakness, or general inability to responsibly handle an automobile. This is a particularly painful situation because giving up a car means giving up a great deal of freedom.

"<u>General forgetfulness</u>. I do not mean the usual forgetfulness which we all experience in our daily lives. I mean a
more <u>consistent</u> forgetting of name, address, phone number,
meal times and so on, forgetting to pay bills and failing
to keep most appointments.

"<u>Extreme suspiciousness</u>. This is a bit more difficult to
pinpoint because everyone may appear to be paranoid occasionally. This paranoia is a persistent suspicion, a fear
of the world at large, and of the people with whom your
parents come in frequent contact. If your parents believe
that their neighbors, friends, family, postman, deliveryman,
doctor, lawyer, hairdresser, landlord and so on are all
conspiring against them, chances are there is some thought
disorder. Intense ungrounded fears about dire consequences
may be a danger signal.

"<u>A series of small fires in the kitchen or bedroom</u>. This
may occur as one dozes during the day, forgets to turn off
the stove, or is careless about electrical appliances or
matches. There may be a series of burned areas in the bedroom, including much of the bedding, or burned areas in
the kitchen. Your parent may be experiencing blackouts
and dizzy spells. These signs are important if your
parent smokes.

"<u>Bizarre behavior of any kind</u>. For instance, dressing in
heavy gloves and overcoat in 90 degree weather, or going
out of doors in frigid weather with no shoes or socks.

Occasionally, men or women expose themselves or act or
speak in a non-characteristic way. Some older people may
hoard food in dresser drawers or clothes hampers.

"<u>Disorientation of a highly consistent nature</u>. Such as
not knowing who one is, or where one is, or who the family
is, or conversing with people who are not there--not being
in touch with reality.

"To sum up, if your parents are no longer able to take care
of themselves in a reasonably safe way, are not well fed,
are not usually in touch with reality, and are not taking
medication as ordered, you, your parents, and your siblings need to discuss what your concerns are and what the
options are. You may want to consult with your parents'
physician as well.

"Most of the time, your parents will be able to participate
in any planning or decision making. As much as possible,
your parents' wishes need to be respected. However, if
your parents can no longer remain in their own home in
spite of all the support systems you and your family can
pull together, the next step may be to consider a move.

"A move may mean:
    Into your home,
    into a sibling's home,
    into an apartment for elderly,
    into a small apartment near your home,

into a nursing home, or

into a hospital for evaluation prior to a move.

"Most people are under the impression that the highest percentage of people over age sixty-five live in nursing homes.
The fact is that only a very small percentage, about 10 percent of those over sixty-five years old, live in nursing
homes.[1] The remaining percentage live in their own homes,
or with family. It is also reassuring to know that although
there is a small percentage (5 percent) of alienated and
isolated elderly, the vast majority of people over sixty-
five years of age do have regular and consistent contact
with their families.

"When you and your family have weighed all of the factors
and are unable to plan for your parents to remain at home,
you will want to be as well-informed about residential or
nursing homes as possible. The material in the packets
distributed earlier will provide you with an excellent base
from which to begin your search for the right place. If
you and your family need to consider a nursing home, and
you have narrowed your choices down to two or three, make
a visit to each of the homes and get a 'feel' for the way
in which the residents are cared for. Talk to the families
of some of the residents to learn as much as possible about
the care and services. Whenever possible, following

_____

1. Data based on findings of the National Jewish Population Studies,
October 1974, from the Council of Jewish Federations and Welfare
Friends, Inc.

placement plan to bring your parent to your home for dinner and family celebrations on a regular basis.

"Too often, families believe that parents in a nursing home must remain there all of the time. If it is physically possible, do plan to take your parents out as often as you can.

"If you decide that the best plan is for your parents to move into your home, plan carefully and in advance with all of your family. The best arrangement is to provide a separate bedroom and bath for your parents' use. Work out in advance who will do the cooking, laundry, household chores, whatever the financial arrangements will be, and what times and days your siblings will be involved to share the responsibility. Having a parent move into your home can work successfully, although it will mean changes for all concerned. Such a new arrangement can bring pleasure and an added richness to your family's life. But as in most life situations, the new arrangement will require patience, understanding, respect, and a great deal of loving kindness."

B. Discussion
The group members will begin to deal directly with their own parental situations and sound out their fears and concerns about the decisions to be made. This can be a very helpful session as members begin to articulate what has been of major concern to them for sometime. This discussion often

138

provides the basis for solid decision making and coming
to terms with the reality of the parental situation.

V. HOME ASSIGNMENT

Remind the group that next week is the last session.

"One of the best things we can do at this point in our lives is to determine what our interests and skills are and explore and develop them so that they may flower and be available to us in our later years. Think about three things which you consider potential interests and strengths for the future. We will begin the session next week by asking each of you to share these three interests and strengths."

Members may have suggested a party for a portion of the sixth session; if so, finalize these plans during closure.

HANDOUTS

FOR

SESSION 5

TWELVE CHARACTERISTICS

Likes my friends

Can do things for me, financially, socially and so on

Is in reasonably good health

Is neat and clean, makes a "good appearance"

Has her own friends and enjoys a full social life

Is able to get along independently and be in charge of herself; can make her own decisions capably and well

Loves and accepts me and my family unconditionally, lets us know we are "okay"

Is a good parent and grandparent

Fun to be with, good conversationalist, current and knowledgeable

Is financially independent

Doesn't interfere in my life or become too critical of my life style or make demands of me

Good advice giver and someone to whom I can turn when I need help and understanding

1. _____

2. _____

3. _____

4. _____

5. _____

6. _____

7. _____

8. _____

9. _____

10. _____

11. _____

12. _____

WHEN IS IT TIME TO CONSIDER A CHANGE IN YOUR PARENTS' LIVING ARRANGEMENTS OR LIFESTYLE?

The Danger Signals

If only one or two of these signals are present, it is probably not significant; however if several are present, or the one or two that are may be life-endangering, it is probably time to consider a change in your parents' living arrangements.

Sudden weight loss

Failure to take medication or overtaking medication

Burns or injury marks on body

Deterioration of personal habits

Increase in car accidents

General forgetfulness

Extreme suspiciousness

A series of small kitchen or bedroom fires

Bizarre behavior of any kind

Consistent disorientation

SESSION 6

SESSION 6

BRIEF OUTLINE

OBJECTIVE: To tie together any loose ends.
To restate the major themes.
To review the goals of the group.
To discuss continuation options and end on a positive note.

PREPARATION

    A. Setting the Stage
    B. Materials Needed
    C. Time Allotment

   I. WELCOME AND UPDATE

  II. GO-ROUND OF THE THREE INTERESTS AND STRENGTHS

 III. REVIEW OF THE GOALS FLIPCHART

 IV. WORKSHOP THEMES REVIEWED

  V. EXERCISE

 VI. WRITTEN EVALUATION OF WORKSHOP

    HANDOUT

SESSION 6

PREPARATION

A. Setting the Stage
    1. Prepare handout copies evaluation forms
    2. Prepare copies of the Goals Flipchart which you prepared in
        Session 2.

B. Materials Needed
    Paper and pencils

C. Time Allotment
I.	Welcome and Update	10 minutes
II.	Go-round of the Three Interests and	
	Strengths	15 minutes
III.	Review of the Goals Flipchart	15 minutes
IV.	Mini-lecture . . . Themes Reviewed	15 minutes
V.	Exercise	15 minutes
VI.	Written Evaluation Form	10 minutes
	Handout and Closure	10 minutes
		90 minutes

You may choose to extend this last session somewhat to allow time
for socializing after the session.

SESSION 6

I. WELCOME AND UPDATE

Briefly outline what you expect to cover in today's session, and
if your group is planning a party, mention that you will close
the formal session and then socialize.

Present your options to the group in response to their requests
for continuation. This is a good time to explain that the group
has been an educative rather than a therapy group, and that
education groups are necessarily time-limited as this group
has been. Your concern about continuing is that the group might
move into becoming a therapy group. The group can discuss this
and you can respond according to your own wishes and capabilities
to continue with them in this new way. The author's experience
is that it is probably wisest not to continue as a therapy group.

II. GO-ROUND OF THE THREE INTERESTS AND STRENGTHS

Ask each member to share the three areas of interest or
strengths and potential skills which he or she can develop for
the later years. This is a particularly good way to help the
group deal with personal growth and planning for the future.
This may be valuable in that group members can begin thinking
ahead for their later years and developing ideas about second
careers, interests, hobbies, and skills. Allow time for
discussion and response.

III. REVIEW OF THE GOALS FLIPCHART

A. Put up the Goals Flipchart (from Session 2) and go over
    it point by point and ask group members as you read each
    point if they believe that it has been covered suf-
    ficiently. This is an important feature of the workshop
    and is a tangible way of illustrating what you've
    accomplished together. The group will enjoy commenting
    on how much they've learned and shared with each other.
    You may hear such responses as: "I told my friend about
    this workshop and she wants to be on your mailing list for
    the next one." "This was the greatest thing that's
    happened to me in a long time." Members are very relaxed
    at this point. Allow enough time for discussion about
    stated goals and how they were met. You may comment that
    everyone has learned much together, but learning does not
    end here, it continues as the members use their new skills
    and understanding.

IV. WORKSHOP THEMES REVIEWED

A. Mini-lecture and Brief Review

NOTE: The following mini-lecture summarizes the contents of the workshop and can be used as a handout.

"We've come to know each other in a very special way in our workshop during these past six weeks. We've learned and grown and have found new ways of coping with our problems.

"In summary these are a few of the major themes of our workshop:

1. "You have needs and rights as a human being and it is all right to recognize these needs and meet them in order that you can meet your parents' needs in a responsible and loving way.

2. "Yes, we believe that you _do_ have a responsibility for your parents. But, we learned together that you will be responsible for your parents as much as you can, in a loving and warm spirit, if you are free of anger, guilt, and resentment.

3. "The concept of filial maturity implies that the old relationship with your parents has been worked through, perhaps resolved, and that you and your parents 'forgive' each other for whatever caused pain to you both in the past. As a person who has achieved filial maturity you can hold your own, meet your own needs, set proper limits and give real help to your parents

without feeling overwhelmed or overpowered.

4. "Aging brings changes, physically and emotionally. Aging will change us, too. It is important for us to be understanding, patient, and loving and very important to communicate and articulate that love (if it can be done sincerely) and to physically express love to our parents by smiling at, touching, stroking, hugging, holding, and kissing.

5. "Learn to talk to your parents as adult children. Express your feelings and wishes and learn to listen to what your parents say and to be sensitive to what they feel.

6. "Let your parents know that you will not abandon them, and that they can count on you when they need you, and that you will be part of their lives always. Make plans with your parents not for them. Include all of your family in sharing responsibility for parents.

7. "Make your parents part of your lives. Help them to face their aging, illness, and death. Helping your parents to face death, discuss their wishes, fears, and concerns may be one of the greatest gifts you will ever be able to make to them. It will also strengthen you.

8. "You are okay. No one is 'perfect', nor could be. You are entitled to your mistakes and so are your parents. So are your children. So are your friends.

9. "Learn to let go of your children and teach them to relate to you as adult children. Help them to understand the principles of filial maturity.

10. "Think about the future, for yourself, for your parents, for your children, and for your grandchildren.

Plan now for your later years, build in strengths and forces which you will need and can utilize for the future."

You may have additional themes which you can add to those listed above. Allow for brief discussion and comments about the mini-lecture material.

V. EXERCISE

GO-ROUND ON REACTIONS TO THE WORKSHOP

This exercise should be included even if time is short. It
provides an opportunity for each member to express his or her
feelings about what she or he has gained from the workshop
sessions. The leader shares his or her feelings, too. This
go-round exercise is extremely important for each member.
Friendships may have developed among several members and they
may have formed an informal "support" group. Members may suggest
a "check-up" get together in the future. If possible you can
schedule a time for the "check-up" and take responsibility for
convening the meeting.

VI. WRITTEN EVALUATION OF WORKSHOP

Distribute the forms (see page 161) and allow enough time for them to be completed.

VII. CLOSURE

Be sure to say good-bye to each member, and think of something
positive to say to each that relates to what you have observed
of his or her learning and changing.

HANDOUT

FOR

SESSION 6

EVALUATION OF WORKSHOP

Name of workshop: _____ Dates: _____

Did the workshop meet your expectations?   Yes _____ No _____

Did the workshop cover the stated topics and
respond to your stated goals?   Yes _____ No _____

Did the leader: Help you to express your concerns?   Yes _____ No _____

Provide appropriate information for
you?   Yes _____ No _____

Help you to consider new ways of
looking at your problems?   Yes _____ No _____

Hear what you said?   Yes _____ No _____

Would you recommend this workshop to others?   Yes _____ No _____

Was the fee appropriate?   Yes _____ No _____

What would you want added to a future workshop on this subject:

_____

What would you want eliminated? _____

What other kinds of workshops would you be interested in? _____

How did you learn about the workshop? _____

Do you know of workshops on this topic being given at other agencies? _____

Why did you choose this workshop? _____

Suggestions and comments about workshop and/or leaders: _____

_____

_____

BIBLIOGRAPHY

BIBLIOGRAPHY

Abernathy,Jean Beaven. <u>Old is not a Four Letter Word: New Moods and Meanings in Aging</u>. Nashville: Abingdon Press, 1975.

Achenbaum, W. Andrew. <u>Old Age in the New Land</u>. Baltimore: Johns Hopkins University Press, 1978.

Becker, Ernest. <u>The Denial of Death</u>. New York: Free Press, 1974.

Bellak, Leopold, M.D. <u>The Best Years of Your Life: A Guide to the Art and Science of Aging</u>. New York: Atheneum, 1975.

Berezin, Martin and Cath, Stanley. <u>Geriatric Psychiatry: Grief, Loss and Emotional Disorders in the Aging Process</u>. New York: International Universities Press, 1965.

Bloom, Lynn Z.; Coburn, Karen; and Pearlman, Joan. <u>The New Assertive Woman</u>. New York: Dell Publishing, 1975.

Brody, Elaine. "The Aging Family." <u>Gerontologist</u> 6:4 (December 1966).

Bucchieri, Therea. <u>Keep Your Old Folks at Home</u>. New York: Alba Books, 1975.

Bumagin, Victoria E. and Hirn, Kathryn F. <u>Aging is a Family Affair</u>. New York: Thomas Y Crowell, 1979.

Busse, Ewald W. and Pfeiffer, Eric. <u>Behavior and Adaptation in Late Life</u>. New York: Little, Brown, 1969.

Butler, Robert H. <u>Why Survive? Being Old in America</u>. New York: Harper and Row, 1975.

Butler, Robert N., and Lewis, Myrna. <u>Aging and Mental Health</u>. Saint Louis: C.V. Mosby, 1977.

Cumming, Elaine and Henry, William. <u>Growing Old: The Process of Disengagment</u>. New York: Basic Books, 1961.

Davitz, Joel and Davitz, Lois. Making it From 40 to 50. New York: Random House, 1976.

de Beauvoir, Simone. A Very Easy Death. New York: Warner Books, 1973.

Dickinson, Peter. The Complete Retirement Planning Book. New York: E. P. Dutton, 1976.

Dienstfrey, Harris, and Lederer, Joseph. What Do You Want To Be When You Grow Old? New York: Bantam Books, 1979.

Donahue, Wilma. Education for Later Maturity. New York: Whiteside Morrow and Co., 1960.

Dorfe, Nancy. The Dying Person and the Family. Pamphlet No. 485, 1975. Public Affairs Pamphlets, 381 Park Avenue South, New York, New York 10016.

Ellison, Jerome. Life's Second Half: The Pleasures of Aging. Old Greenwich, Conn.: Devin-Adair Company, 1978.

Erikson, Erik. Childhood and Society. Particularly, Chapter 7: Eight Ages. New York: W. W. Norton, 1963.

Finkelhor, Dorothy. The Triumph of Age: How to Feel Young and Happy in Retirement. Chicago: Follett Publishing, 1979.

Franzblau, Rose N. The Middle Generation. New York: Holt Rinehart and Winston, 1979.

Goleman, Daniel. "We Are Breaking The Silence About Death." Psychology Today, September 1976.

Harris, Louis, and Associates, Inc. The Myth and Reality of Aging in America. Washington, D.C.: National Council of the Aging, 1975.

Irwin, Theodore. After Sixty-Five: Resources for Self-Reliance. Pamphlet No. 501, 1973. Public Affairs Pamphlets, 381 Park Avenue South, New York, New York 10016.

Lambert, Richard. "Political Consequences of Aging." 1974. American Academy of Political and Social Science, 3937 Chestnut Street, Philadelphia, Pennsylvania 19104.

Laslett, Barbara. "The Family as a Public and Private Institution: An Historical Perspective." _Journal of Marriage and the Family_ 35:3 (August 1973).

Neugarten, Bernice, ed. _Middle Age and Aging_. Chicago: University of Chicago Press, 1968.

Norback, Craig T. and Norback Peter G. _The Older American's Handbook_. New York: Van Nostrand Reinhold, 1977.

Poe, William D. _The Old Person in your Home_. New York: Charles Scribner's Sons, 1969.

Potthoff, Harvey H. _Loneliness: Understanding and Dealing With It_. Nashville: Abingdon, 1976.

Puner, Martin. _To the Good Long Life: What We Know about Growing Old_. New York: Universe Books, 1974.

Rosow, Irving. _Social Integration of the Aged_. New York: Free Press, 1967.

Saint-Exupery, Antoine De. _The Little Prince_. Trans. Katherine Woods. New York: Harcourt Brace, 1943.

Satir, Virginia. _Peoplemaking_. Palo Alto, Calif.: Science and Behavior Books, 1972.

_____. _Self Esteem_. Milbrae, Calif.: Celestial Arts, 1970-1975.

Shanas, Ethel and Streib, Gordon F., eds. _Social Structure and the Family: Generational Relations_. Englewood Cliffs, N.J.: Prentice Hall, 1979.

Simos, Bertha. "The Relation of Adults with Aging Parents." _Gerontologist_ 10:2 (Summer 1970).

Smith, Elliott Dunlop. _For Those Growing Old and Those Concerned with Them_. New York: Barnes and Noble, 1972.

Smith, Manuel J. _When I Say No, I Feel Guilty_. New York: Bantam Books, 1975.

Spicker, Stuart F.; Woodward, Kathleen M.; and Van Tassel, David D., editors. <u>Aging and the Elderly: Humanistic Perspectives in Gerontology</u>. Atlantic Highlands, N.J.: Humanities Press, 1978.

Stern, Edith M. and Ross, Mabel. <u>You & Your Aging Parents</u>. New York: A. A. Wyn, 1953.

Streib, Gordon. <u>The Changing Family: Adaptation and Diversity</u>. Reading, Mass.: Addison-Wesley, 1973.

Taylor, Robert. <u>Welcome to the Middle Years</u>. 1976. Acropolis Books Limited, Colortone Building, 2400 17th St. N.W., Washington, D.C. 20009.

Troll, Lillian, Israel, Joan, and Israel, Kenneth, eds. <u>Looking Ahead: A Woman's Guide to the Problems and Joys of Growing Older</u>. Englewood Cliffs, N.J.: Prentice Hall, 1977.

_____; Miller, Sheila; and Atchley, Robert. <u>Families in Later Life</u>. Belmont, Calif.: Wadsworth, 1979.

Viorst, Judith. <u>It's Hard to Be Hip Over Thirty and Other Tragedies of Married Life</u>. New York: New American Library, 1968.

West, Jessamyn. <u>A Matter of Time</u>. New York: Harcourt Brace, 1966.

Zinberg, Norman, and Kaufman, Irving. <u>Normal Psychology of the Aging Process</u>. Rev. New York: International Universities Press, 1977.